Round-the-World Flight
10-14 July 1938 · 3 days 19 hours

Fairbanks
Minneapolis
New York
Paris
Moscow
Omsk
Yakutsk

REGD

Page 49 (Record Flight)

TWA 1940

San Francisco
Fresno
Las Vegas
Boulder Dam
Los Angeles
Winslow
Phoenix
Albuquerque
Amarillo
Wichita
Kansas City
St. Louis
Chicago
Indianapolis
Dayton
Columbus
Fort Wayne
Harrisburg
Pittsburgh
Philadelphia
New York
Newark

REGD

Page 50 (Airline Ownership)

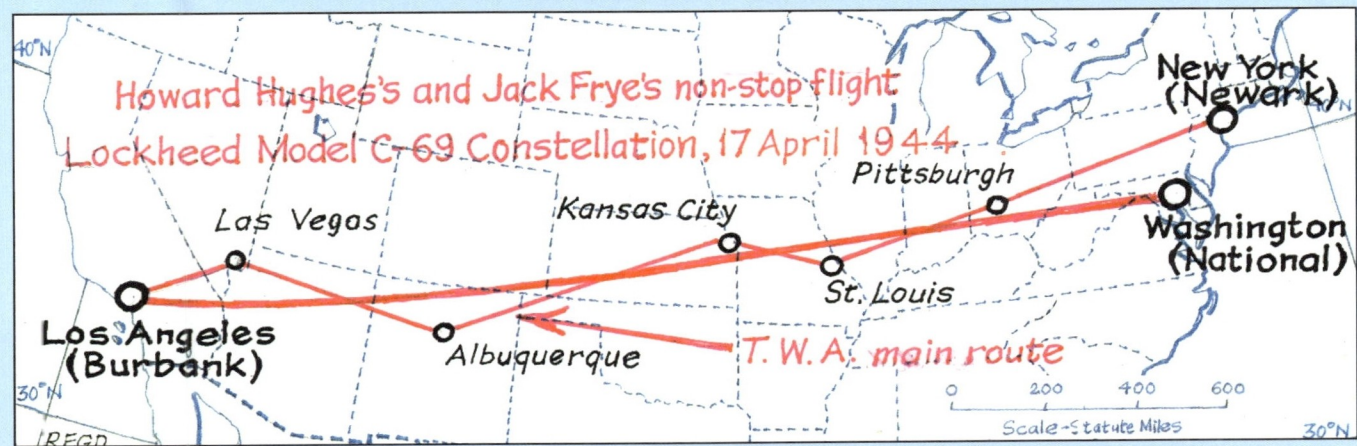

Howard Hughes's and Jack Frye's non-stop flight
Lockheed Model C-69 Constellation, 17 April 1944

40°N
New York (Newark)
Las Vegas
Kansas City
Pittsburgh
Washington (National)
St. Louis
Los Angeles (Burbank)
Albuquerque
T.W.A. main route
30°N
30°N

0 200 400 600
Scale - Statute Miles

REGD

Page 52 (Constellation Delivery and Record)

HOWARD
HUGHES

An Airman, His Aircraft, and His Great Flights

Other Pictorial Books by Paladwr Press

Great Airlines of the World
An Airline and its Aircraft Series
by R.E.G. Davies, illustrated by Mike Machat

Lufthansa: An Airline and Its Aircraft
Aeroflot: An Airline and Its Aircraft
TransBrasil: An Airline and Its Aircraft
TWA: An Airline and Its Aircraft
Eastern Air Lines: An Airline and Its Aircraft
British Airways — The Imperial Years
(Regrettably, Pan American, Delta, Saudia, no longer in print)

Specials
by R.E.G. Davies, illustrated by Mike Machat

Lindbergh: An Airman, his Aircraft, and his Great Flights
Berlin Airlift: The Greatest Humanitarian Airlift
(with John Provan)
Comet: The World's First Jetliner
(with Phil Birtles)
The Chelyuskin Adventure
(with Yuri Salnikov)

HOWARD
HUGHES

An Airman, His Aircraft, and His Great Flights

Thomas Wildenberg
R.E.G. Davies

Paladwr Press

To Anne and Marjorie
For their continued support and encouragement.

Published by Paladwr Press, 1906 Wilson Lane, #101, McLean, Virginia 22102-1957, USA

Manufactured in Singapore

Aircraft Drawings, Maps, and Charts by R.E.G. Davies

Technical Editing by John Wegg

Detailed Layout by Liz Weaver

ISBN 1-888962-27-5

First Printing

Contents

Color drawings of the airplanes are indicated by the titles in blue.
Route maps are indicated by page numbers in red.

Howard Hughes had good reason to appear self-satisfied after his victorious debate before the special setnate committee.

Foreword

The popular film *The Aviator* was notable for the way in which Howard Hughes's piloting skills and aviation achievements were emphasized, rather than other well-publicized aspects of his eventful life. I did, however, observe that, well though he acted the part, Leonardo DiCaprio was not the Howard Hughes that I knew. Physically, Howard was taller, his voice was deeper; and his personality was more complex. I can state this with some authority, as I knew The Aviator for 31 years, as his flight engineer and co-pilot. I was one of the very few of his working associates with whom he was on Christian name terms.

I was his flight engineer on the notorious mile-long close-to-the-surface flight at Long Beach by the Kaiser-Hughes HK-1 giant flying boat. I know that he fully intended to clear the waves, rather than make another taxi test, as he discussed every detail of the whole procedure with me hours beforehand. When he decided to make the take-off, he turned towards me, where I was in charge of the engine and fuel settings, and said "give me all you've got." I did, on all eight engines.

Howard Hughes has been described in countless magazines and newspapers, as well as in several books, as a rich playboy. In his early years, this was true, but he was many other things as well. He was a fine pilot, and knew the technical details of all the many airplanes that he flew. Many a designer who followed his sometimes detailed instructions discovered that he was invariably correct. After his near-fatal crash in the XF-11, he was never quite the same, and in his fast-declining years, he became eccentric. When in London, he fell down the hotel stairs and broke his hip, but refused to have it properly fixed, and this could not have helped. Ultimately, his senility was marked with strange obsessions and even stranger personal habits. Howard's shortcomings in later life have too often outweighed an appreciation of his considerable achievements as an airman.

Flying beside him in the right hand seat for many years, I can assert that although his judgement, even his self-discipline, could occasionally be questioned, his skills as a pilot were superb. The oft-quoted reference to his preference for wearing sneakers, of even flying with bare feet, and his choice of casual attire, was as much for comfort as for appearance. Every aircraft is an individual machine, and Howard was always conscientious in acquainting himself with their special features before he took off. He digested every page of the manufacturers' manuals, and in the case of aircraft that bore his name, it could be said that he helped to write them — except the big helicopter, which I wrote.

While many of his nights were spent with beautiful women, many of his days, at least during the late 1940s and the 1950s, were spent in designing, modifying, advising, and even working on airplanes, as well as flying them. I believe that he never really loved any woman, although he must have had a high respect for Katherine Hepburn, who could match his spirit and intellect. But he really loved airplanes, and he loved aviation.

His character as a whole was a strange mixture. During the years when I knew him, he was alternately an introvert and an extrovert. He often travelled — and almost lived — incognito, as much to avoid the attentions of the paparazzi as to avoid public recognition. On the other hand, he did not mind being awarded several trophies for his achievements, culminating in a ticker-tape parade in New York. He was a bon viveur, yet he enjoyed snacking at a lunch-bar or diner — for which he never paid personally; the establishment was always reimbursed later. Like royalty and aristocrats, he never carried money. His initials were H.R.H., or His Royal Highness, which must have amused him. If he was amused, he did not often show it. He was essentially a loner, and he did not tell jokes or play games with others.

Owning almost everything that he was involved in, airplanes, houses, hotels, films, manufacturing plants, he was a take-charge man. He never imposed his authority on others in an over-bearing manner, but you always knew who was boss. He fired some of his top executives, but it was a tragedy when Ralph Damon died, as they made a fine team at T.W.A., and Hughes seemed to have lost his way thereafter. As for me, I could make suggestions on the flight deck, to which he would reply "Chal, you don't know what you're talking about!" But later on, without mentioning the matter, I would notice that he had taken my advice.

The sub-title of this book includes the word Great to describe his flights. I would add that same word also to Airman and Aircraft, as the account in these pages justifies those adjectives. The authors have performed an essential service to aviation literature by putting the record straight in chronicling the many achievements of a truly great airman.

Chalmer Bowen, March 2006

Chalmer Bowen was the flight engineer on the well-publicized maiden (and only) flight of the Hughes HK-1.

Introduction

The Real Story

My writing experience has so far comprised monographs, magazine articles, and a few books on the subject of naval operations, and especially commentaries on the use of aircraft as an essential arm of the United States Navy. During 1998 and 1999, I was privileged to be the Ramsey Fellow at the Smithsonian's National Air and Space Museum, and although I concentrated on my chosen marine curriculum, I became, almost as a therapeutic diversion, interested in other aspects of aviation endeavor.

One of the books that I picked up was *Rebels and Reformers of the Airways*, and I became acquainted with its author, Ron Davies. In the book, one of the outstanding men who was the subject of the book's essays was the famous (or notorious, depending on individual opinion) Howard Hughes. Until I read this book, I shared the common judgment of the man as a rich playboy who consorted with Hollywood film stars, who managed to fly a large flying boat, and who declined in his latter years in some form of chronic illness. The Hughes chapter in this book was something of a revelation: Hughes was a great airman.

This led me to search for other evidence of his airmanship — and hidden in the pages of several books that took the traditional route to readership popularity, I did find many references. But these seemed to be marginal to the main themes of sensationalism. One source was in Dr. Bill Leary's compendium of profiles of great names in commercial airline history. The contribution on Howard Hughes was, once again, by Ron Davies, who obviously respected, even admired his achievements in the air, rather than in bed.

I was surprised, when I started to "beat the bushes" for further evidence of Howard Hughes's aviation career, that in spite of wide publication, many of his greater accomplishments, except the "Spruce Goose" flying boat flight, had seemed to have been forgotten or overlooked. Perhaps the seal was set on my desire to write a book about Hughes the aviator, rather than the rich playboy, by the appearance of the movie film, *The Aviator*.

And so I approached Ron Davies to see if yet another book could be written and published about this aviator. As in the film, the theme would be aviation, his first love, possibly even above his love of women, and possibly transcending any preoccupation with his own great wealth. This book is the result.

Thomas Wildenberg

Publisher's Note

When Tom Wildenberg approached me with his customary enthusiasm, I realized that this was just the kind of subject that Paladwr Press should embrace with equal dedication. We set out to accomplish this work, an activity that quickly developed into a partnership — which it always should be, rather than the master-and-servant approach which is too often the case.

I was struck immediately by the opportunity to produce a book that parallelled the Paladwr book on Charles Lindbergh. This was written and produced in 1997, the 70th anniversary year of that airman's historic non-stop solo flight across the Atlantic Ocean. The motivation behind its publication was the lack of recognition by the media — newspapers, magazines, radio, and television — of anything else that Lindbergh did in a career of pioneering advocacy of popular airmindedness. Certainly, the great flight deserved to be handsomely remembered, but little was reported, even marginally, about his technical contributions to the inauguration of the U.S. transcontinental air route or to his tran-oceanic flights that were the aerial pathfinders for the great Pan American Airways.

The sub-title of the Lindbergh book was thus *An Airman, His Aircraft, and His Great Flights*, and Tom's approach not only impressed me with its raison d'être, but also because it was a perfect match, even to the sub-title, of the previous one. The parallels were several. Both were great airmen — Hughes's piloting skills were often forgotten — and in their own ways, their technical expertise and confirmation launched complete aircraft generations.

As to the lack of recognition of the range of accomplishments, my scepticism was confirmed by a little market survey, during which I asked dozens of people, mainly those in the aviation community, who might be expected to know more about Howard Hughes than could be gleaned from the popular press. I was surprised — to put it mildly — to learn that few, no more than five percent, could identify any of his great flights, not even those for which he was awarded prestigious trophies, nor the one for which, like Lindbergh, he was honored with a ticker-tape parade down New York's Broadway,

This book takes its rightful place in the series of pictorial books in which Paladwr Press aims to combine an accurate text with complementary illustrations that enhance and enliven a fascinating narrative. This is a biography of a truly great airman.

R.E.G.Davies

Acknowledgements

We would like to thank several fellow-researchers for their assistance in compiling this tribute to Howard Hughes. Greg Harbaugh, President of the Florida Air and Space Museum, provided access to the Howard Hughes collection for graciously allowing us to reproduce photographs from the Museum's collection. Museum volunteers Ernie Sanborn, Joyce Sanborn, and Imma Burka gave us valuable assistance with that collection. Similarly, Kevin Logan gave us help with the Albert Lodwick Collection at the Lakeland Public Library. Staff members of the National Air and Space Museum, Dan Hagedorn, Dom Pisano, and Bob Van der Linden, gave guidance and assistance. Matt Rodina was responsible for the details of the B-23 fleet.

Photographs were donated to the project by Chalmer Bowen, who, as a close associate of Hughes (see his Foreword to this book) was able to provide valuable insights into Howard's character and personality, confirmed previous facts and opinions, and added a few choice stories. Tom Northrop sent us rare pictures taken during the production of *Hell's Angels*, Robin Dunn completed details of Howard's affair with the Bristol Britannia, and Roger Bentley drew from his personal collection.

A special acknowledgement is due to Liz Weaver, our graphic designer, who often doubled as an editorial copy-editor, and whose work was a vital component in the production of this book. And, as always, to long-time colleague John Wegg, who ensured technical accuracy.

The Airman

It has been said that the difference between a
"pilot" and an "aviator" is that a pilot is a technician,
and an aviator is an artist in love with flight.

A Complex Life

History has not always been kind to Howard Hughes, who is often remembered as an eccentric, philandering, reclusive billionaire. Few people realize that he was one of America's greatest aviators. In the remarkably short span of 12 years — between 1935 and 1947 — Hughes built and flew the world's fastest landplane, captured numerous transcontinental speed records, circumnavigated the globe by air in record-setting time, and oversaw the construction of what, at the time, was the largest airplane in the world. He served as his own test pilot for that huge flying boat and was the only man ever to fly it. He was the only American to have twice been awarded the annual **Harmon Trophy** as the world's best aviator. He received the prestigious **Collier Trophy** for significant achievement in the advancement of aviation; and was honored by Congress, which awarded him a special medal in recognition of his round-the-world flight of 1938. During his remarkable career, Hughes produced and directed *Hells Angels*, one the greatest aerial film classics of all time. He was instrumental in creating the **Lockheed Constellation**, the most advanced airliner of the post-war era of piston-engined landplanes. He transformed one of American's first domestic airline companies (Transcontinental & Western Air) into a worldwide giant, having renamed it **Trans World Airlines (T.W.A.)**; and established one of the leading aerospace companies of the 20th Century (**Hughes Aircraft**). In 1966 he became America's first billionaire when, in just twenty minutes he sold his stock in T.W.A., worth $546,549,171.

The Aviator

Hughes was captivated by flight at an early age. By the time he was twenty-three, he had inherited a considerable fortune, had earned his pilot's license, and had purchased his first airplane. He qualified as a transport pilot a few years later and was even briefly employed as a co-pilot for American Airlines. It was the only paid employment that Hughes ever held.

Although he was a skilled pilot, Howard could be reckless at times. He liked nothing better than to push his airplanes to their limits. Usually they responded, but not always. He was involved in no less than six airplane crashes or mishaps, one of which came very close to killing him. He was never satisfied with the airplanes that he purchased and was always trying to improve their performances. He enjoyed creating mechanical things and was never more at ease than when he was around airplanes. He loved everything about them.

The Visionary Engineer

He was also a visionary airman who was never afraid to experiment with new or unconventional approaches to aviation. He had an engineering-oriented mind and this was matched by a proficiency for all things mechanical. Those who knew him well contend that he had all the attributes of a successful engineer and had more in-born engineering ability than most people gave him credit for. He had a "human engineering touch," according to Lockheed president Robert Gross, and he was especially knowledgeable concerning aircraft systems and instrumentation. But he was the type of person who could never accept anything on face value. He had to research it himself or experience it personally.

The Introvert

This remarkable man was often shy and introverted, but always self-assured and self-interested. While he often appeared aloof and out-of-touch, he could also be witty and extremely sharp-tongued when the occasion demanded it. He could be arrogant or charming, thoughtful or inconsiderate, forgiving or vengeful. When he was in the air, he was an entirely different man from the one whom people knew on the ground. The only time he felt comfortable with others (except perhaps with his many girl friends) was when he was around other airmen. Unlike most men, he never had a close personal friend or a lifetime "buddy." Howard Hughes was a loner.

He was an obsessive perfectionist who developed a single-minded fixation on whatever it was he desired, to the total exclusion of everything else, including other people's feelings or inconvenience. Most of all, he had a fanatical compulsion to control every aspect of his life and immediate environment. He had the instincts of genius but often lacked the self-discipline required to exploit such flashes of inspiration. Like a spoiled child, he insisted on acquiring anything that was denied him. The image of money was the channel that eventually etched Howard Hughes's name into the public mind, not his aviation prowess. In later years, and except for his association with "The Spruce Goose" — a title that he hated — his name called forth visions of untold wealth, eccentricity, and a gift for turning everything he touched into gold.

Aviator: Howard Hughes the Aviator, from a painting by Robert Tananbaum on display at the Hughes Medical Institute, Bethesda, Maryland.

Growing Up

His Father, Big Howard

Howard Robart Hughes Jr. was born on Christmas Eve 1905 in the family's small frame house at 1404 Crawford Street, a few blocks east of what is today's downtown Houston. Hughes Sr., better known as Big Howard, was a tall flamboyant man who endowed his son with a flair for the dramatic. At the time of young Howard's birth, he was a wildcatter and oil speculator; a man who lived by his wits and spending whatever he had whenever he could get it.

When little Howard, or "Sonny," as he was called by his family and friends, was three years old, his father acquired the rights to a rotating drill bit that he and a partner had developed and patented. This revolutionary drill bit could go through rock like butter. Consequently the Hughes Tool Company revolutionized the oil prospecting business and the drill bit quickly turned into an endless pot of gold for Howard Hughes Sr. and his son. Big Howard lived a lavish lifestyle thereafter, traveling around the country in a private railroad car, entertaining his prospective clients with extravagant dinners and expensive gifts. He was away most of the time, leaving Sonny in the care of his mother.

His Mother, Allene Gano

His mother, **Allene Gano Hughes**, was a tall thin woman of quiet sophistication. She was the daughter of a Texas judge and her Huguenot ancestry included men in the revolutionary and civil wars. Allene Hughes was an overly protective, doting parent who exerted an overpowering influence on her son's early development. She was obsessed with his physical and emotional well-being. She worried continually about Little Howard's health and what she perceived to be his super-sensitivity, his nervous nature, and his inability to make friends easily with other children. Her fears became so ingrained into his physical and mental well being that they would subconsciously affect Howard for the rest of his life.

The Electric Bicycle

As a child, Howard Hughes was precocious, inventive, and tremendously persistent. He was a quiet shy boy who did not make friends easily and who spent a great deal of time alone. Instead of concentrating on school work, he preferred to tinker with mechanical gadgets that he disassembled and put back together in the workshop that his father had created for him behind their house. Even when young, he was allowed to amuse himself with bits of wire and metal, inventing curious objects that only he could understand. One of his greatest thrills was to construct a makeshift radio, which he assembled from various household items, including a doorbell.

Young Howard's interest in all things mechanical mirrored that of his father, who encouraged his son's mechanical leanings, hoping to inspire him to study engineering. Even so, when Big Howard refused to buy a motorcycle for his son, Little Howard converted his bicycle into a motorbike, using a starter motor and battery scavenged from a local junkyard. The invention brought brief notoriety to the budding engineer when a photograph of the motorbike and its youthful inventor appeared in the local Houston newspaper.

As a teenager, Howard Hughes Jr. became increasingly interested in the burgeoning technology of radio, whose blooming during the 1920s mirrored the computer craze that would inflict millions of teenagers decades later. With his best friend he built a radio with which the two boys used to broadcast their own radio show to the local neighborhood. Later, he built a short-wave ham radio that he operated under the call sign 5CY. Hughes's early interest into this developing technology would continue beyond his teenage years and would be put to good use in future aviation projects.

Howard Hughes Senior as he appeared in the 1913 directory, Men of Affairs of Houston.

Young Howard with his mother, Allen Gano Hughes.

Howard and his box camera.

Howard's electric bicycle. (Houston Public Library)

Howard's First Flight

School Days

Howard's formal education was erratic. He attended a number of local schools until he was fourteen years old, when he was sent to the prestigious Fessenden School in West Newton, Massachusetts. Big Howard hoped that the schooling that his son received at Fessenden would prepare his son for Harvard University, where he and his father before him had attended. While a student there, Hughes was active in school activities. He played the saxophone with the jazz band, was a bench warmer on the football team, wrote for the school paper, and was runner-up in the school's golf tournament. His fellow students and teachers remembered him as an intelligent, quiet, shy, and retiring person, who could be witty when the stimulus was great enough. Although his grades improved, he was not an enthusiastic student. He much preferred to spend his time on the school's nine-hole golf course, where he was found practicing when his father visited the school in the late fall of 1920. Defying school rules, Howard Sr. spirited his son off to see the Yale-Harvard boat crew races that were held annually on the Thames River at New London, Connecticut. In these somewhat unusual circumstances, Howard Hughes Jr. was first introduced to flight.

Howard at fifteen while a student at Fessenden School

Blind Date with an Airplane

The Yale-Harvard Regatta was a widely-publicized social event for alumni that Big Howard could not pass up. A loyal Harvard fan rooting for the Crimson, he promised his son that if Harvard won the race, the boy could have whatever he wanted. When his alma mater achieved this goal, Big Howard was obliged to pay up.

On the way into New London, the younger Hughes had seen a seaplane tied up to a bulkhead in the Thames River, next to a large sign that advertised airplanes rides for five dollars each. The airplane, a **Curtiss Seagull** (see next page), belonged to the Piper-Hudson Seaplane Service and was being operated as a local sightseeing and tourist attraction. Like many boys of his age, Little Howard wanted wings. He yearned to emulate those special heroes of the day — the much-publicized "Aces" of the First World War.

The Lure of the Aces

When the fighting began in Europe in August 1914, an air of chivalry still prevailed among flyers and it was not unusual for aircraft from opposing sides — French and British against German — to pass one another while going about their reconnaissance duties. Most of them had flown in the same air meets as the flying enthusiasts and were inclined to wave at each other. But, as the value of aerial reconnaissance became more and more apparent, the camaraderie of the airmen soon dissolved into enmity. Pilots and observers began carrying pistols, rifles, and shotguns for use against their adversaries in the sky. These peashooters were soon replaced by machine guns, which greatly increased the lethality of the airplane. The skill and bravery of the pilots engaged in such aerial combat was acknowledged by the French press, which dubbed them "Aces" — a term that was soon applied to pilots who had shot down at least five enemy aircraft, and which still holds true today.

Little did he know at the time that, only a few years later, he would try to emulate his heroes and, in a civilian context, became an "ace" himself.

Big Howard Helps

Howard's father was not thrilled with his son's request. Although flying was one of the more glamorous forms of amusement in 1920, it was also one of the most dangerous and he did not want his son to break his neck. Young Howard was insistent, however. So he paid the pilot five dollars and the two of them climbed into the cramped cockpit for the ten-minute flight that followed. It was a turning point in Howard Hughes's life. Those few minutes in the air marked the beginning of his lifelong love affair with aviation.

Hughes left Fessenden at the end of the school year and returned to the family home in Houston. That summer, according to some sources, the precocious teenager discovered a barnstorming pilot who was willing to teach him how to fly. Without telling his parents, he enrolled in the first course of instruction that he had ever really wanted to take. He paid for the lessons out of his family allowance, and kept the experience a secret.

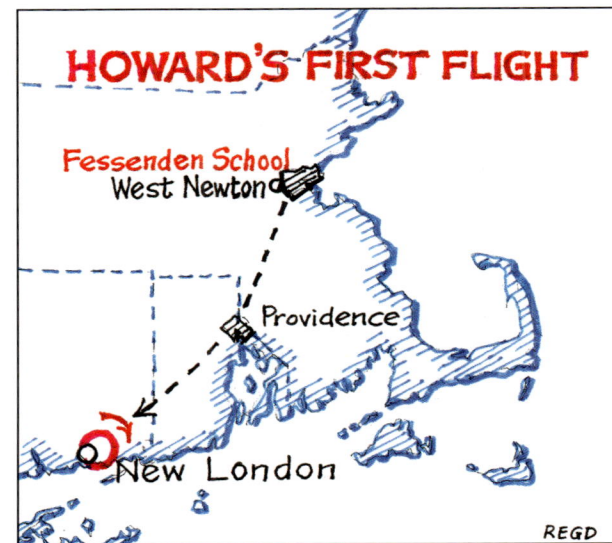

Curtiss Seagull

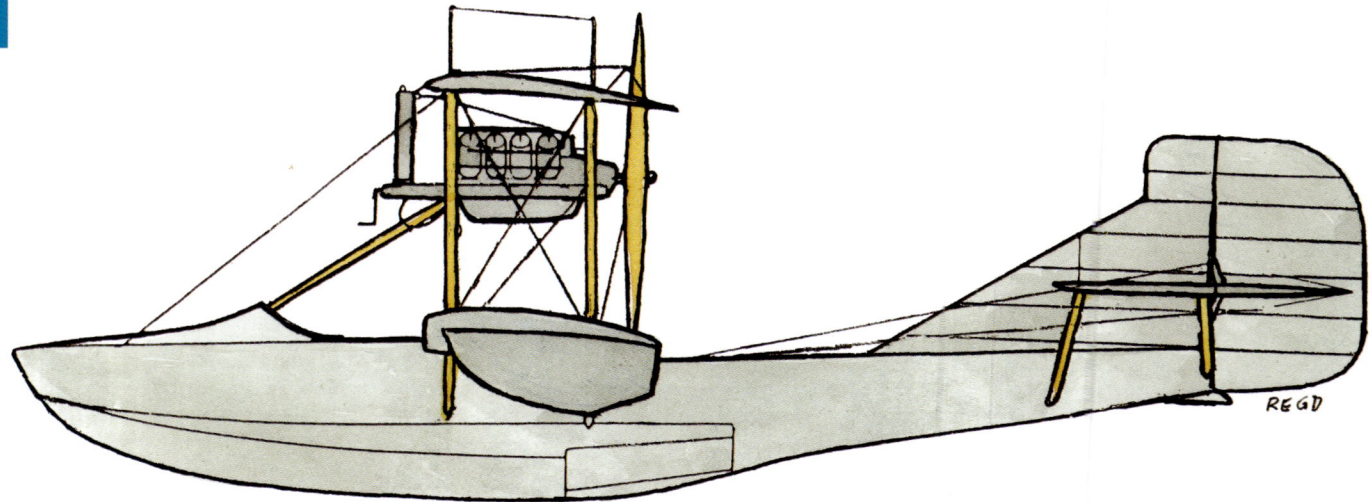

REGD

The Best Flyng Boat

When the Curtiss Seagull was introduced in 1919, many considered it to be the best small flying boat in the world. It was the last in a line of highly successful seaplanes that had started with the Model F-Boat trainer, introduced by Curtiss at the end of 1913. Much of its design was taken from the original Curtiss pusher of 1912, which is generally acknowledged as the first American flying boat. The U.S. Navy bought a large number of F-Boats and used them extensively at Pensacola, Florida, to train naval aviators during the First World War.

Military to Civilian Flying

In 1916, the F-boat gave way to the Model MF (Military Flying Boat), a larger, improved aircraft that incorporated the latest in aeronautical design knowledge. After the War, the MF design was converted into a multi-place Seagull that was designed for the civilian market. Unfortunately, it had to compete with the glut of war-surplus MFs that had found their way onto the market. These "no frills" military models were comparatively cheaper and few Seagull versions were sold.

A similar situation arose after the Second World War, when a glut of surplus Douglas DC-3s (mostly military C-47s and variants thereof), DC-4s (C-54s), and Curtiss C-46s threatened to impede post-war technical development. In this case, however, with "America's secret weapon," Howard Hughes inspired the construction of the Lockheed Constellation, to end any such threat.

Length	29 ft
Wing Span	50 ft
Engine	Curtiss C-6 (160 hp)
Seating	pilot and two passengers
Cruise Speed	60 mph
MGTOW	2,726 lb.
Normal Range	288 miles

Size comparison with Hughes-Kaiser HK4 Hercules (p.74)

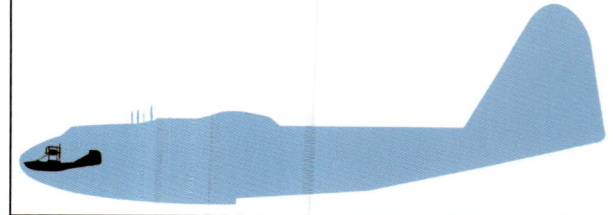

Riches Through Tragedy

Double Tragedy

By the fall of 1921, Big Howard had moved the family to Los Angeles, where he had opened a branch of the Hughes Tool Company to service the booming oil industry in southern California. Instead of sending Howard to some well-known preparatory school in the East, his parents — wishing him to be nearby — enrolled their son into the Thacher School in Ojai, near Santa Barbara. Though Thacher was much smaller and more intimate than his previous school, it had no effect on his shyness, now becoming more apparent. He shunned group activities and spent endless hours alone, usually in the surrounding hills, riding the horse that he had purchased. This solitary activity, often conducted in the remotest of locations, foreshadowed his later proclivity for endless hours of solo flight.

During the spring semester, Howard's thirty-nine-year-old mother died suddenly on 28 March 1923 while undergoing minor surgery at the Baptist Hospital in Houston. Her unforeseen death was a traumatic event for the seventeen year-old teenager. More tragedy was to follow. Only nine months later, on 14 January 1924, his father — the only man in the world whom he wanted to please — suffered a massive heart attack, while he was conducting a business meeting at the company's headquarters in Houston. Big Howard died so suddenly that his son never had a chance to say goodbye to the father whom he admired and loved.

To lose both parents while still a teenager is shattering for anybody. The premature deaths of both parents had a profound psychological effect on Howard Hughes Jr. He had been raised to believe in the delicate nature of his physical well-being and the danger of germs. He became more obsessed with his own health after their deaths and began to believe that he too was destined for an early grave. As a result, he started taking all sorts of precautions that he felt would protect him from disease. This became a life-long obsession that would worsen as the years went on.

The Financial Empire

In his will, which had been drawn up eleven years earlier, Howard Hughes Sr. had left one-half of his estate to his wife and one-quarter to his son. When Allene died, her share of the estate had automatically passed to her son, making young Howard, still a teenager, the major beneficiary. The other quarter was divided between Howard's grandparents and his father's brother, Felix. The estate's only asset of any real value was the company that bore the Hughes name. Hughes Tool Company was worth millions — it was a "cash cow" that was generating several hundreds of thousands of dollars in profits a year, but it was valued at only $750,000 for inheritance tax purposes.

Following his father's death, Hughes spent the first few weeks living in California at the home of his uncle Rupert, who wrote and directed movies. Brooding and sullen, at the age of nineteen, Howard, now stood six foot three inches tall and had grown into a handsome young man. Rupert, who had previously shown no particular interest in his nephew's welfare, now contrived to have himself appointed Howard's guardian. If Rupert's intent was to maneuver himself into a position to have access to his nephew's considerable wealth, he was sadly mistaken. When Howard found out about his uncle's plans, he packed up his golf clubs and moved back to the family home in Houston.

Howard Takes Over

He wasted no time in taking control of both his life and his money. "I would never be able to get along with my relations — Hughes later explained — and that's why I determined to buy them out and go it alone." His relatives were not eager to sell, but Hughes somehow convinced them to part with their shares in the company, which he purchased on 24 May 1924, only four months after his father's death. The Hughes Tool Company (or "Toolco," as it would frequently be called during the years that followed) and its immense capacity to generate cash was now the sole property of Howard Hughes. Having secured complete, unfettered control of this father's company, Howard turned his attentions to securing his personal sovereignty over the corporate affairs at the Hughes Tool Company. He was not yet twenty years old.

Even at that young age, and unlike most youngsters when ending their years of education, young Howard knew exactly what he wanted to do with his life, and even made a declaration, most informally, not on the proverbial "back of an envelope," but on the equivalent.

To achieve this ambition, Howard could reflect on the old axiom: money isn't everything, but it helps.

The Hughes Tool Company ("Toolco"), shown here with its founder, Howard Hughes Senior, the ultimate source of Howard Jr.'s wealth. Source: Houston Public Library.

Things I want to be,
1. The best golfer in the world.
2. The best ~~flyer~~ pilot.
3. The most famous producer
of moving pictures.

Howard Hughes's goals written on the back of a receipt from Foley's men's clothing store on 5 January 1925. He started to write "flyer," then crossed it out adding the word "pilot."

Ambition Unfettered

Through the Courts

Under Texas law, a minor such as Howard Hughes could petition the courts at age 19 to remove the legal restrictions of a minor so that he could be declared an adult. Howard probably learned this from his golfing companions at the prestigious Houston County Club where he was now routinely playing with some of the most prominent men of Houston, including weekly outings with a circuit Judge named Walter Montieth. Throughout the fall of 1924, Hughes campaigned persistently with the judge to act favorably on his request. On 24 December, the day when he turned nineteen, Hughes filed a petition in Judge Montieth's court to have the restrictions of his youth removed. The judge took just one day to consider the request. On the day after Christmas, 26 December 1924, Montieth declared Howard Hughes Jr. to be free "of all disabilities of minority and of full age." Hughes left the court with a confidence that few teenagers of his era could muster. He was tall, good-looking, extremely rich, and enthusiastically inspired.

Steam Car

At nineteen years of age, the world was Howard Hughes's oyster. He had enormous wealth and complete freedom to do what he wanted with it.

Like his father before him, Hughes had no interest in the day-to-day running of the Tool Company. He considered it to be a monument to his father — to be preserved, protected, and left alone. Although, in the long term, he knew that he had other worlds to conquer, Howard still did not have a clear idea of what he wanted to do as a beginning. One of his first ventures was an excursion into the steam-powered car business. The idea proved to be commercially impractical, but Howard had a lot of fun with the prototype. After driving it around town for a while, he would park it next to the curb and casually walk away as the pressure began to build up. When the pressure relief valve would suddenly let go, the ear-shattering noise scared the living daylights out of any passers-by.

Golfing and Flying

In an effort to improve his golf game, Howard joined the Wilshire Country Club and began to play every day with the best golfers he could find. On many of these outings, a local barnstormer would tip the wings of his biplane as he passed over the golfers below. On one of these occasions, Howard copied the airplane's registration so that he could track down the pilot, who usually parked the airplane on the far side of Clover Field, near Santa Monica. Howard went to the airfield, where he found the airplane's owner, a pilot named **J. B. Alexander**. He offered Alexander $100 per day if he would teach him to fly. This was a huge sum at the time, and Alexander readily agreed to begin dual instruction. As Alexander later recalled, Hughes was a good student and a natural pilot.

Howard's steam automobile.

Golf was one of Hughes's earliest passions and he had dreams of being the world's best golfer.

Marriage

His Apprenticeship

Big Howard, an indulgent father, had, when his wife died in 1923, sent young Howard to Europe, with a friend. Dudley Sharp, as a chaperon. He also provided an allowance of $5,000 a month, which in today's money, would be at least the equivalent of $50,000. Young Howard did not keep a diary, but some of it could have been spent on the proverbial "wine, women, and song." It is known that, in Brussels, he started to gamble with $10, worked this up to $10,000, and then lost it in one more spin of the roulette wheel.

Ella Rice

While working on the steam car, he had begun to woo a young woman named **Ella Rice**. He did not waste time, except to go to Europe. They were joined in matrimony on 1 June 1925. It was an arranged marriage that would provide Ella, a Houston socialite related to the founder of Rice Institute, with financial security and social status. For Howard, it provided sexual companionship and the illusion of maturity and stability.

After the wedding, the couple left for New York for a three-month honeymoon that involved sightseeing, shopping, and sailing on Long Island Sound. They returned to Houston in October. They stayed just long enough to pack their belongings before heading for Hollywood, where they took up residence in the Ambassador Hotel, just as Big Howard had done several years earlier. Consumed with his own interests, activities, and ambitions, Howard soon found his wife to be clutching and a petty annoyance. He sent her back to Houston where she stayed for several months.

The Playboy

Howard Hughes's relationship with the opposite sex is not the subject of the book, but it cannot be ignored; as for much of his life, his association with some of the world's beautiful women was notorious. Even though, as in the case of Katherine Hepburn, the partnership was between two people of equally strong wills, most of his affairs were brief, impetuous, and appeared to have little depth of emotion. This is not to state that he treated women badly (although Yvonne de Carlo for one would not agree) and sharing his bed was always generously rewarded.

During the early years of his career, he was the epitome of the "tall, dark, and handsome" ideal, cherished by all young ladies. Furthermore he had money to burn, and his companions never had to worry about what his parents would think (as they were dead) or what his brothers or sisters would think (as he was an only child). And so, in between, at first, his golf and, later, his romance with airplanes, he found the time and the inclination for other romances, temporary though they may have been.

His character in later years, after his near-fatal airplane crash, and his apparent increasing concern for his health, led to an introspective mood, leading to a withdrawal from the public eye. But after his first marriage with Ella, he was the quintessential playboy, making no secret of his affairs. His name was linked with almost every famous film star of the 1930s, Lana Turner, Linda Darnell, Bette Davis, Katherine Hepburn, and others. There were many others, film actresses who never became household names, and many other unknowns for whom he kept households. Unfortunately he seemed not to care about what the world thought of his sexual morals — if he ever thought about them — and he was so rich that there was never a penalty for what, in ordinary family circles, would be regarded as loose living. As far as is known, he was not a churchgoer.

Hughes vs. Lindbergh

Also — again, as far as is known — he never had children. And this makes an interesting comparison with his contemporary, the great aviator, **Charles Lindbergh**. Charles was not a playboy; he was respectably married, with children; without the blatant, almost exhibitionistic, profligate habits of Hughes. Yet he too strayed from the "straight and narrow" conduct of married life.

The two great airmen together make a fascinating subject for character analysis and comparison. Both seemed to be married to their obsession: aviation. Hughes would live to break records, Lindbergh to trail-blaze for the airlines; yet both contributed in their own ways to the advancement of commercial aviation. Both were unfaithful to their wives, one the extrovert, the other clandestinely. But such was their individual genius that the world has forgiven their shortcomings.

Hughes's first wife, Ella, taken just after the couple had been married.

Howard Makes Movies

First Picture

Like his foray into the nuances of Texas majority law, Howard's initiation into the movie-making business began on the golf course. On one of his daily outings he was introduced to a successful young actor named **Ralph Graves**. Like many actors then and now, Graves wanted to move behind the camera. He had a story about a Bowery bum with a heart of gold who kept bumping into all sorts of unusual and dire predicaments that he felt would make the subject of a good picture. Graves persuaded Howard to invest in the movie, which was titled *Swell Hogan*. It was budgeted at $50,000, but cost more than $80,000 to produce. The finished product was so bad that Howard ordered the projectionist to burn the film and it was never shown or distributed.

Settling In

The debacle surrounding Hughes's first attempt at movie-making had little, if any effect, on his new-found determination to became a famous movie producer. Within weeks, he embarked on another project suggested by **Marshall Neilan**, an old friend of uncle Rupert's. Neilan was a well-established director who had many contacts in Hollywood. Once again, the project had got off the ground after a chance meeting in the golf course's clubhouse, the so-called "nineteenth hole." After a short discussion about his latest project, the seasoned director enticed Hughes into producing his next picture, *Everybody's Acting*. The film, budgeted at $150, 000 made more than $75,000 for the Caddo Company, a subsidiary of the Hughes Tool Company, whose charter had been amended to allow Howard to make movies with it. The film's financial success solidified Hughes's determination to become firmly established in the film-making business. His third movie, a comedy set in the trenches of the First World War, titled *Two Arabian Nights*, was a radical departure from the low budget films he had previously made. The movie cost $500,000, generated $640,000 in profit, and garnered considerable acclaim when it won an Academy Award for its director.

The Micro-Manager

Hughes's next movie, *Hell's Angels*, was nothing if not ambitious, and was the first example of how, if he undertook any project, he always did so in a big way. The film would celebrate on a grand scale the deeds and valor of the airmen of the First World War of 1914–18. The inspiration for the plot coincided with Charles Lindbergh's famous trans-Atlantic flight from New York to Paris in the spring of 1927. The solo non-stop crossing in a single-engined airplane captivated the nation and created a public fervor for airplanes and aviation. This mood did not go unrecognized by the inspiring producer, who eagerly sought to capitalize on the excitement created by Lindbergh's spectacular accomplishment. Neilan agreed to direct the picture, and a team of scriptwriters was put to work on the story line about two brothers in the Royal Flying Corps and their romantic rivalry over a licentious socialite.

Howard quickly became preoccupied with every aspect of the film. It became the focal point for all his activities and energy. No detail was too trivial for his involvement and no decisions about anything could be made without his approval.

Personality Conflicts

Ella Rice became the first casualty of Hughes's obsession with making the film. After the success of *Everybody's Acting*, he abandoned their temporary abode at the Ambassador Hotel in favor of an expensive house rental that was more suited to his growing reputation as a producer. After a day at the studio, he would lock himself into the downstairs study, which had been transformed into an office, bedroom, and sanctuary. Ella was forbidden to enter. He had no time for romance and zero tolerance for her whining ways.

Neilan was the second casualty. By late August, the director was so fed up with Hughes's interference that he walked out of the studio, slamming the door behind him. Hughes replaced him with **Luther Reed**, an aviation enthusiast and former aviation editor of the *Herald Tribune*, then under contract to Paramount. Reed could not get along with Hughes either. He walked out in disgust on the last day of September, shouting: "If you know so much, why don't you direct it yourself?" Hughes accepted the challenge, telling **Noah Dietrich**, his business manager "I'll keep a director on the set, but the decisions will be mine." Howard Hughes was, even then, the quintessential micro-manager.

The Director

Hughes was in the director's chair when shooting of the indoor scenes began on 31 October 1927. He had spared no expense in assembling a set of props and a film-making crew on a magnitude that was impressive even by Hollywood standards. During the next two months, Hughes kept dozens of cameramen busy shooting the same scenes over and over again. One sequence showed the crew of a German Zeppelin leaping to their deaths to lighten the ship so that it could be saved. The crewmen, played by Hollywood stuntmen, jumped from a mockup of the ship's gondola that was suspended high above the stage. Hughes ordered eighteen mattresses to be placed under the gondola's hatch and studied the sequence as each of the thirty stuntmen jumped onto the mattresses, one by one. He ordered the scene reshot over and over again until it had been filmed more than a hundred times.

The Perfectionist

Hundreds of other aerial scenes were shot before Hughes would approve them. He was totally involved in making the air sequences and spent hours in planning the airplanes' routes and camera angles. For realism, Hughes insisted that all aerial scenes had to be shot against a backdrop of white, puffy clouds. Southern California, with its wall-to-wall sunshine, had none to offer, so he moved a production crew of a hundred people and dozens of airplanes further north to Oakland. After six months of training, and waiting for the perfect cloud patters to emerge, he filmed a spectacular air battle involving scores of fighter airplanes of the First World War's western front. This single film footage extract was destined to become a masterpiece of cinematography.

Incidentally, a flair for portraying dramatic action was not the only example of Hughes's instinctive film artistry. As the second half of *Hell's Angels* begins, the slow emergence of the nose of a Zeppelin from impenetrable fog is a masterpiece of suspenseful foreboding.

Hell's Angels

On His Own

While Hughes was in Oakland, waiting for the clouds to appear, Ella pined away in Los Angeles. She finally threw in the towel on 1 October 1928. Shut out of Hughes's life, she quietly went home to Houston and started divorce proceedings. The marriage could never have succeeded, for Howard was too much of an individualist to share life with anyone, at least permanently. Later on, he shared some of his days and nights with many other women, but only on a temporary basis, and there was little depth in their companionship. He was too obsessed with his personal preoccupations and consuming ambition.

The "Talkies"

He had planned to release *Hell's Angels* in 1929, but the introduction of sound — the "talkies" — which made its sudden appearance with Al Jolson's *Jazz Singer* in October of 1927, made the silent film obsolete, almost overnight. Although he had already invested more than $2 million in the film — an enormous sum for a movie at that time — Howard Hughes was not going to have his name attached to a silent film when sound had abruptly become the new sensation. He would scrap all the dramatic scenes already filmed and reshoot the movie with sound. The aerial scenes could be saved by injecting sound effects. This added another $1.8 million dollars to the film's cost, making it the most expensive film ever made when it was released in 1930.

Howard Creates a Star

The invention of the talkies resulted in several acting casualties, those of both sexes who were good looking but far from good talking. Hughes replaced Greta Nessen, the film's leading lady, whose foreign accent was unacceptable, with a bit-part actress named **Jean Harlow**. She was, with Howard's promotion, destined to become one of Hollywood's early sex symbols. This was the first time when he created a movie star, but it would not be the last. Undoubtedly the ladies had to be prepared to make concessions but Howard always regarded these as a fair trade.

Howard Assembles His Crews

Throughout the spring and summer of 1927, Hughes's scouts scoured the United States and Europe, looking for airplanes that had flown on the Western Front in the First World War. He wanted the aerial shots for *Hell's Angels* to be as realistic as possible. Characteristically the perfectionist, he knew that the only way to achieve this was to use authentic wartime aircraft. He had the money to obtain them; and to produce the aerial scenes, Howard bought or leased 87 vintage airplanes at a total cost of $562,000. Of these, 37 were Allied SPADs, Sopwith Camels, SE-5s, and the German Fokkers, all of which had seen service in the war. The others were modified and painted to look like warplanes.

Hughes assembled this aerial armada at Mines Field — the present site of Los Angeles International Airport — and hired 70 pilots to fly for his private air force. His first recruits were novice pilots, hired for $10 a day. After they cracked up three of the film's airplanes in quick succession, he hired professional pilots at $200 a week – $50 more then he paid the actress Jean Harlow for her starring role. The pilots were kept busy, shooting the same scenes over and over again, in an effort to satisfy Hughes's quest for realism. His incessant striving for perfection often bordered on recklessness. In one scene, he ordered a fighter to fly so low that it hit one of the cameras on the ground. A ground crew of 150 men had to be on hand to service and repair any of the aircraft that were damaged during the filming.

As Hughes's air force grew, he moved its operations to a large plot of land that had been leased in the San Fernando Valley at Van Nuys. Named **Caddo Field**, it was turned into the replica of an American airfield in France. The field served as the main base of operations for the *Hell's Angels* air force and as a background for the ground operations of the Allied squadrons in the picture. Another field was acquired near Chatsworth, where a German airfield, called the Jolly Baron's Nest, was re-created to serve as the home of Baron von Richthofen's Flying Circus. Smaller fields were leased at Inglewood, Encino, Santa Cruz and San Diego.

Hell's Angels stunt pilots line up before the largest fleet of airplanes of the 1914–18 World War ever assembled for the making of a motion picture. The event took place on the runway of Oakland Airport, 15 March 1929. (Air Force photograph)

Howard's Private Air Force

(left) Plotting an aerial sequence for Hell's Angels with Harry Perry, chief cameraman.

(right) A few of the Hell's Angels team pose for the camera, at Oakland, where, for Howard, the clouds were better than in Los Angeles. (Tom Northrop collection)

Harry Perry, complete with parachute, prepares for action at Oakland. (Tom Northrop collection)

The Howard Hughes Air Force, posed in front of the modified Sikorsky S-39, complete with machine gun and gruesome skull insignia.

Waco Whirlwind

Howard's First Airplane

The Waco was the most popular airplane in America when it was purchased by Howard Hughes for his personal use during the filming of *Hell's Angels*. It was easy to fly, it had good take-off performace, climbed rapidly, and had excellent landing characteristics. Introduced early in 1927, the Model 10 was an improved version of the highly popular Model 9. The 10 had a larger cockpit than the 9, came with an adjustable stabilizer, had more wing area, and had better overall performace. It was one of the first commercially-available airplanes to be equipped with a shock-absorbing landing gear outfitted with "oleo" struts. The version purchased by Hughes was powered by the highly-reliable Wright J-5 Whirlwind engine, the same as the one used by Charles Lindbergh to cross the Atlantic, in May of the same year.

Student Pilot

After shooting for *Hell's Angels* began in the fall of 1927, Hughes began to take dual flight instruction in a serious way from **Charles LaJotte**, a 22-year-old Army-trained aviator, fresh out of the National Guard. Wanting to get as much dual instruction as possible before he soloed, Hughes never mentioned his previous flying lessons. "He was there to learn all he could from me" explained LaJotte. By December Hughes had passed the written examination for his private pilot's license and had successfully flown his check ride with a C.A.A. inspector in the Waco. His pilot's license was issued on 7 January 1928.

As Howard gained additional flying experience, he was able to qualify for additional C.A.A. ratings. He received his tranport pilot's license on 24 October 1928 and continued to upgrade it, increasing his ratings until he was fully qualified to fly any multi-engined aircraft, weighing 7,000 lb. or more over land and sea.

Length	31 ft
Wing Span	23 ft
Engine	Wright J-5 (220 hp)
Seating	2, Tandem
Cruise Speed	85 mph
MGTOW	2,025 lb.
Normal Range	525 miles

Size comparison with Constellation (p.55)

The Wright J-5 Whirlwind on a Waco 10.

A Waco Model 10, similar to the one flown by Howard Hughes in the 1920s. All the Waco series of biplanes were very popular during the late 1920s and the 1930s, as they flew well and, because they were slow and manueverable, they were very "forgiving".

Howard's First Crash

The Gotha

The filming of *Hell's Angels* was wrought with accidents and crashes that took the lives of four of the film crew's airmen. The most notorious and tragic of these involved Roscoe Turner's famed **Sikorsky S-29A**, which had been disguised to resemble a **German Gotha** bomber. In his continuing quest for realism, Hughes leased the twin-engined airplane for $11,000 and had it modified and painted in German colors, together with appropriate insignia that included a German cross on the tail and a grim skull on the fuselage. To simulate the rear gunner's position, his special effects team added a machine gun to the open cockpit, fashioned a false cockpit in the front of the cabin, and placed fake machine gun positions in the nose and cabin entrance.

The script called for the Gotha to be spinning out of control before crashing into the ground in a spectacular crash. None of the pilots on the set would perform the dangerous stunt, that required the fragile bomber to be placed into a diving, power-on spin, until Hughes offered a $1,000 bonus to **Al Wilson**. One of the most experienced pilots on the set, Wilson agreed to fly the stunt that required him to pull out of the spin behind a hill, as explosions were set off on the ground simulating a fiery crash.

Tragedy

Wilson and **Phil Jones**, a mechanic who volunteered to set off the smoke pots that would make the aircraft look as if it was on fire, climbed aboard the big bomber on 22 March 1929. Both were fitted with parachutes in case of an accident. As Wilson took off from Caddo Field, he was followed by three camera planes and Hughes in his Waco. Wilson, who had never flown the S-29A before, must have changed his mind, once he got the feel of the big airplane.

After taking the airplane through a few mild diving turns, he put the S-29A into a medium-angle spiral and signaled Jones to activate the smoke before ordering him to bail out. Wilson leaped from the cockpit and landed safely, but Jones, located deep within the cabin, apparently did not hear the order to bail out. The order was probably just a shout, and above the roar of the engines, could not have been heard more than a few feet away. Phil started the smoke-making gear and released several lamp-black canisters before the Sikorsky slammed into the ground, killing him instantly.

The Gotha, of course, was a complete write-off, the loss of which was not covered in Hughes's contract with Roscoe Turner — who was never compensated for the loss.

Crack-Up

Hughes's quest for perfection bordered on recklessness to the extent that it almost cost him his own life. It was said that he would not ask the pilots to do anything that he would not do himself. When **Frank Clarke**, one of the film's stunt pilots, balked at the idea of making a left hand turn immediately after take-off in the Thomas Morse Scout, Howard jumped in the cockpit. He had never flown the Scout before and was unfamiliar with the difficult handling characteristics induced by the extreme torque of its rotary engine. [Note: the Gnôme-Rhône rotary engine revolved with the propeller to which it was attached by a fixed crankshaft.]

Nevertheless, he started the engine, adjusted his goggles, took off, gained a few hundred feet in altitude — and against the advice of his fellow pilots — banked sharply to the left. Pilots, stuntmen, and mechanics watched in horror as the airplane spun into the ground. After the crash, the public relations department put out a story that Hughes had crawled out from the wreckage unhurt, but he was unconscious and had to be rushed to the hospital where he underwent facial surgery to repair his crushed cheekbone. Uncharacteristically, Howard is said to have admitted to Clarke, "You were right."

The Sikorsky S-29 owned by Roscoe Turner in "civilian dress" before it was disguised to look like a German Gotha.

Thomas Morse Scout after Howard Hughes's first crack-up.
(Florida Air Museum)

Accolade

A Flair for Publicity

The premier showing of *Hell's Angels* revealed Hughes's instinctive flair for publicity. He promoted the film on a scale that was in keeping with its extravagant cost of $3.8 million. For the film's premier, Hughes leased Grauman's Chinese Theater, a lavish edifice on Hollywood Boulevard that was dedicated to the movie industry which appealed to the public's incurable craving for opulent extravagance. He covered the entrance portal with huge signs bearing the letters HELL'S ANGELS in red neon. Searchlights in the overlooking Hollywood Hills bathed the theater in colored lights. The marquee was embellished by a huge likeness of Jean Harlow, dressed in a strapless gown, and alluringly caressing Ben Lyon's cheek. An authentic Fokker fighter graced the theater's entrance court, and the replica of a Sopwith Camel was painted on the theater curtain. Hollywood Boulevard was lined with arc lights projecting vertical columns of light skyward. Replica aircraft hung above the crowds while squadrons of real airplanes zoomed overhead.

The movie opened on 30 June 1930. It dazzled audiences and critics alike. It was a triumph that Hughes would remember as the best night of his life. He had completed the most expensive film ever made without the help of a major studio; and had orchestrated an opening night that would never be equaled in terms of its complexity or captivating effect. A celebrity overnight, Hughes was aged only 24 — even younger than Charles Lindbergh when he made the 1927 flight.

Financial Wiz

As the story of *Hell's Angels* unfolded in the Press, Hughes's role in its production was embellished, giving him more credit than was his due. He was proclaimed as a daring, independent producer, blessed with the "Midas Touch." The film never recovered its staggering production cost, but Hughes's publicity people advertised the movie as an incredible money-making success, claiming a profit of more than $2 million. This was a myth, but the alleged commercial prosperity of *Hell's Angels* catapulted Hughes in the eyes of the public and into the ranks of the financial wizards of American big business. Dated though it is, the film is still ranked as one of the classics of all time.

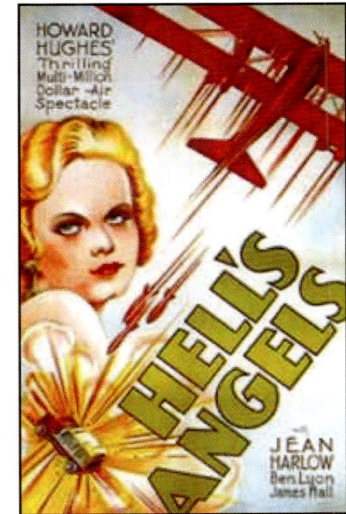

Opening night at Grauman's Chinese Theater.

Aerial Adventures

End of the Movies

Hughes continued to make moving pictures until 1932, when his reckless spending, combined with the Great Depression, exhausted the profits of the Hughes Tool Company. The U.S. economy had hit rock bottom that year, and for the first time since its founding, the Tool Company failed to generate a profit. This brought Howard into contact with his ex-wife Ella. Unable to come up with the $250,000 instalment on the 1929 $1,250,000 divorce settlement, Hughes had to renegotiate the agreement, extending the payments until 1939. To guarantee these, he was prohibited from producing any new movies until the settlement was complete. This forced him to close the Caddo Company offices and to sever his contracts — though not his personal contacts — with movie stars and directors.

True Love: Flying

Ever since he had received his first pilot's license, airplanes had provided him with a relaxing — though sometimes dangerous — escape from early business and social pressures. He loved nothing more than to take off from Burbank on a leisurely flight that carried him north over the San Gabriel Mountains, turning east over the high deserts, then south towards Palm Springs, west to the coast, which he followed until he reached Los Angeles, where he made another course change to bring him back to Burbank.

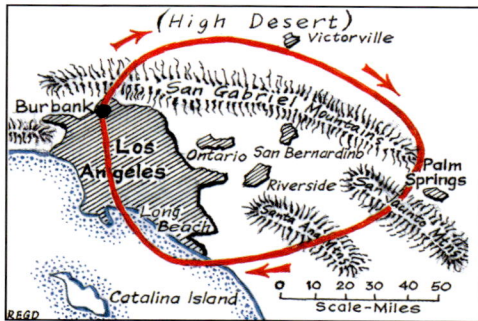

Howard Hughes's practice course was not exactly straightforward. It involved three ranges of mountains, hot and high conditions in the California high desert, and navigation across a densely-populated area.

The Fokker F-10 tri-motor was a successful airplane for T.A.T., which merged with Western Air Express to form T.W.A. Its career ended after the disastrous crash at Bazaar, Kansas, in 1931.

Howard Hughes handling passenger baggage while working for American Airlines in 1932. (Florida Air Museum)

American Airlines Co-pilot

Hughes disappeared for two months during the summer of 1932. His action was to add to his aerial knowledge and skill by flying, under the assumed name of Charles W. Howard, as a crew member for American Airways. He made his first flight on 8 July 1932, occupying the right-hand seat as the co-pilot on the route from Los Angeles to Phoenix. Before long he was assigned to the Fort Worth-Cleveland run, at what was then, for ordinary mortals, an excellent salary of $250 a month. In addition to his flying duties, Howard helped passengers with their luggage and happily collected boarding passes. The work introduced Howard to airline operations, meteorology, and navigation. It was superb training while it lasted. He was fired after three weeks when the airline discovered that he was not Charles Howard and had falsified his identity and credentials. Working as a pilot for the airlines was the only salaried job that he ever held, and did nothing to help his divorce settlement. But the experience must have been marvelously therapeutic.

Sikorsky S-38 Amphibian

Executive Flying Boat

After returning from his stint as a co-pilot, Hughes's pilot's license had been upgraded to a multi-engine rating, and he used the proceeds from the sale of half-dozen airplanes left over from *Hell's Angels* to buy a Sikorsky S-38 amphibian. He ordered the airplane with a special interior that was outfitted with a leather divan along one side of the cabin. After taking delivery of the $59,000 aircraft on 4 January 1933, Hughes had it sent to the shops of Pacific Aeromotive in Burbank, where it was extensively modified to his demanding specifications. The job was handled by a young mechanic named **Glenn Odekirk**. Hughes spent a lot of time in the hangar, talking shop with the mechanics as the work progressed. The two men got along well together, and Glenn was soon hired by Hughes to be his personal mechanic.

Cross-Country Odyssey

As soon as the modifications were finished, Hughes and Odekirk climbed aboard the S-38, and took off on a series of cross-country adventures that ended at the Sikorsky plant near Bridgeport, Connecticut. Hughes left Odekirk with the airplane and traveled to New York City where he took a suite in the Drake Hotel. Whenever he wanted to fly, Howard would telephone Glenn in Bridgeport before boarding the train for the one-hour ride from New York. While Hughes was on the train, Odekirk readied the Sikorsky for flight.

Hughes spent most of the summer of 1933 in New York and flying — usually with a budding starlet on the leather divan — over and around Long Island Sound, visiting various transitory friends and acquaintances. The glamorous pilot, with his youthful good looks, great wealth, and flamboyant reputation as a moviemaker, made him a much- sought-after guest on the estates of the wealthy.

The First Sikorsky Amphibian

The S-38, the first Sikorsky flying boat to be produced in quantity, made its maiden flight in September 1928. It was a highly successful airplane for its day and it helped to pioneer airline routes and was frequently used for exploration. It was popular with private owners especially the wealthy, who could afford to have their airplanes fitted out with luxurious

accommodations, leading to the S-38's sobriquet of "The Explorer's Air Yacht."

Caribbean Pioneer

In 1929, Lindbergh flew a Sikorsky S-38 around Central America and the Caribbean, pioneering future air routes for Pan American Airways. The versatile little craft carried eight passengers, and lightly loaded, could fly over a range of about 500 miles, though it was usually confined to stages of much shorter distances. Pan American operated a fleet of 39 S-38s. Juan Trippe head of Pan Am, and Howard Hughes's great competitor, also flew frequently in the S-38.

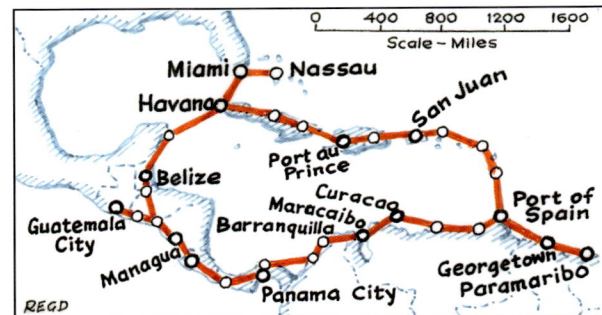

Length	40 ft
Wing Span	72 ft
Engine	2 x Pratt & Whitney R-1340 (420 hp)
Seating	Crew 2, Passengers 8–10
Cruise Speed	110 mph
MGTOW	10,480 lb.
Normal Range	600 miles

Size comparison with Hughes-Kaiser HK-1 Hercules (p.74)

The Sikorsky S-38 was the aircraft chosen by Charles Lindbergh for Pan American's pioneering route around the Caribbean in 1928.

Speed Seekers

"There is no excuse for an airplane unless it goes fast."
—Roscoe Turner

Air Races

Throughout the modern age, men and women have continually challenged one another to see who could go faster, further, or higher. As the technology of aviation began its rapid advance in the 1920s, speed, distance, and other record-setting flying events began to capture the imagination of the American public. The excitement mushroomed after Lindbergh's flight across the Atlantic, which initiated a media frenzy. The names of air racers, record setters, and aerial explorers were splashed across the newspaper headlines, while their exploits appeared in the newsreels.

By the early 1930s, air racing was one of the biggest sports in America. They were sponsored by well-intentioned entrepreneurs who offered thousands of dollars in prize money during the money-tight Great Depression. The money, coupled with the notoriety that could be achieved by winning a major race, was a great incentive for aircraft manufacturers to create better and faster airplanes. Like the colorful pilots who flew them, the aircraft too became famous: names like Wedell-Williams, the Gee-Bee, and the Hall Bulldog became household words. The best of the racers were highly streamlined monoplanes equipped with the largest engines available.

Hughes Enters the Field

While Howard Hughes indulged himself in the S-38 with the pleasures of flying, not to mention a few creature comforts, he was instinctively attracted by the excitement of speed in the air. He was more than interested in air racing. His approach was simply that he had to be the best. Howard's first racer had been a highly modified Boeing Model 100A that the Caddo Company had acquired from the Boeing Company in July 1929. The airplane was a two-place civilian counterpart of the Army's P-12B pursuit plane. It had been purchased through a "special arrangement" that enabled the fighter to fall into Hughes's hands. The 100A provided Howard with invaluable experience in high-performance aircraft. He enjoyed the thrill of the airplane's power and he flew it often until the early part of May 1931, when he sent the gawky-looking biplane, with its un-cowled engine and conventional landing gear, to the

Unusually smart (he must have had a date that evening) Howard Hughes was proud of his new racing airplane, a Boeing 100A, the inspiration for the design of which he could take full credit.

Douglas Aircraft Company. He issued clear-cut instructions to turn it into a streamlined racer.

Tight Money

Once again, Howard's lust for perfection reared its ugly head as he made a pest of himself at Douglas. He stopped in constantly, at all hours, making changes, disrupting work, and inspecting parts that he knew nothing about. Time and money seemed to mean little to him as the request to do it over became a common joke around the plant. When the remodeling was complete, he refused to pay the huge charges — as much as $75,000 according to some reports — that had been rung up. Howard had wagered his mechanical instincts against conservative or traditional technology. Donald Douglas was no mean a competitor himself, but presumably wrote the affair off to experience. This special customer eventually offered to settle the bill for $15,000, which Douglas unhappily accepted.

The only known image of Howard's Boeing 100A as it appeared, with cowled engine, and still lacking fairings for the landing gear, after leaving the Douglas factory. (Florida Air Museum.)

24   *Howard Hughes*

Boeing 100A

If You Don't At First Succeed...

Dissatisfied with the Boeing s performance, Howard cast about for another manufacturer who could make the airplane go faster. In November 1931, he took the modified Model 100A to the Lockheed Aircraft Company in Burbank, California, where it was placed into the hands of **Dick W. Palmer**. A 1925 graduate of the California Institute of Technology with an M.S. in Mechanical Engineering from the University of Minnesota, Palmer had entered the aircraft business in 1929 as a draftsman for Lockheed and had quickly risen to become its chief engineer. When Palmer was finished, Hughes's Boeing 100A had been transformed into a sleek, single-seat biplane racer with every conceivable aerodynamic improvement. These included a landing gear that was elaborately streamlined by fairings and spats, and a long-chord N.A.C.A. cowling over a highly souped-up Pratt and Whitney 450-hp engine. A streamlined headrest — necessitated by the additional forward area created by the cowling and the landing gear — was also faired into the taller vertical fin and rudder assembly.

Mission Accomplished

On 5 March 1933, flying the streamlined racer over a measured course at Mines Field in Los Angeles, Hughes had it officially timed at 212.39 mph. It then sat in a hangar for the rest of the year while he was gallivanting across the country in his Sikorsky amphibian. The next nine months must have included quite a lot of gallivanting, for it was not in Howard's nature just to sit around. At all events, by the end of the year, he turned his attention back to his first love, and embarked on a mission to achieve one of the goals that he had first written on the back of a clothing store receipt in 1925.

All-American Air Races

The All-American Air Races at Miami Beach had been established in 1929, to be held in January each year as a winter exercise from the doldrums that aviation usually experienced at that time of year. In addition to the races, which took place over a 5- mile triangular pylon course, the event included all the usual air show activities.

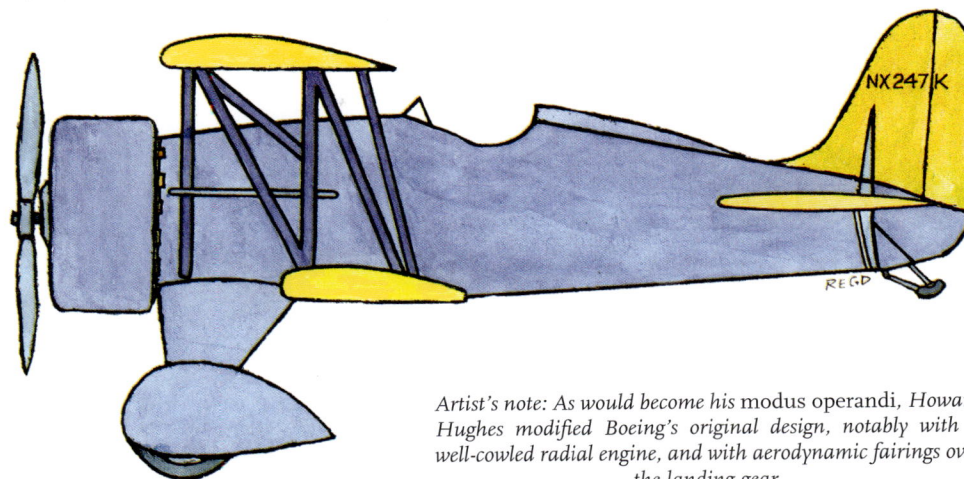

Artist's note: As would become his modus operandi, Howard Hughes modified Boeing's original design, notably with a well-cowled radial engine, and with aerodynamic fairings over the landing gear.

Length	20 ft
Wing Span	30 ft
Engine	Pratt & Whitney R-1340-9 (525 hp)
Seating	1 pilot
Cruise Speed	212 mph
MGTOW	2,630 lb.

Size comparison with Constellation (p.55)

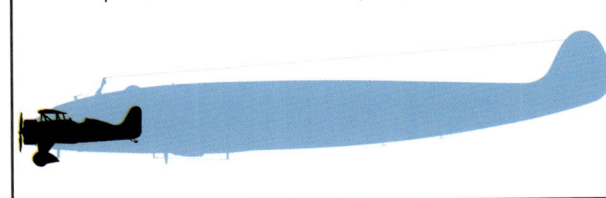

Enter Howard Hughes

After the New Year, Howard had the Boeing racer ferried to Miami Beach for the All-American Air Races. It arrived on 10 January 1934, four days before the Sportsman-Pilot Free-For-All, a closed-course pylon race for amateur pilots, took place. In preparation for the race, Howard had Odekirk tune and tweak the Boeing's 1,344 cubic-inch Wasp engine to its maximum horsepower. On 14 January, with the racer averaging 185.7 mph, he easily won the event, almost lapping his nearest competitor during the 15-mile race over a 3-mile triangular course. Hughes logged a total of 4 hr. 20 min. in the Boeing racer, conducting tests and demonstrations during the air meet.

The Winged Bullet

More Speed

The victory in Miami whetted Hughes's appetite for speed. Although the Boeing 100A had performed well, it was upstaged by the **Wedell-Williams 44** that was demonstrated before the Miami crowd by **James R. "Jimmy" Wedell**, holder of the world's land-plane speed record of 305 mph. Inspired by the success of the Boeing racer and encouraged by Odekirk, Hughes set out to build an even more revolutionary racer. He telegraphed **Dick Palmer** — the highly-talented designer who had perfected the Boeing 100 — asking if he would design and engineer the "fastest plane in the world." Palmer had left Lockheed and was now working for the Airplane Development Corporation. He agreed to take on the special project in his spare time, but was able to devote only a few hours a day to it. As the project progressed and his responsibilities increased, Palmer's boss sensed the overload and told him that he would have to choose one job or the other. The gifted engineer could not turn down the opportunity to design the most advanced airplane in the world. He left Airplane Development and set up shop in a two-car garage in Glendale, California.

While Palmer was working out the preliminary design details, Howard was checking out the latest developments in engine technology. He visited Pratt & Whitney in Hartford, Connecticut, to see what their latest engines looked like and did the same at the Wright Aeronautical plant in Paterson, New Jersey. Although he was "officially" on the East Coast, he would commute back and forth to the West Coast by commercial airliner to oversee the design of his special airplane.

Hughes respected Palmer, who was known for his advanced theories on aircraft design and expertise in aeronautical engineering, and the two men got along well together. After discussing power plants, both agreed on the new, low-frontal area (to reduce drag), twin-row 14-cylinder Pratt & Whitney Twin Wasp Jr. radial engine.

Toward the end of February, Palmer began to hire master wood-workers and experienced aircraft engineers to help build the wind tunnel models that would be used to test out the aeronautical design concepts that would be incorporated into the racer. The hardwood models were all built to a scale of 9/32 inches to the foot. On 20 April 1934, Palmer started

to test models at the 10-foot wind tunnel at Cal-Tech's aeronautical laboratory in Pasadena.

The Hughes Aircraft Company

To build the his "Special" airplane, Hughes leased a building, owned by Charles Babb, located across the road from the Grand Central Airport in Glendale. Palmer and his staff, now increased in numbers, moved into the installation at the end of April. Before the work began, Hughes had a temporary plywood wall erected around the construction area and ordered an armed guard to be on duty during the night. As the work was about to begin, he sent Glenn Odekirk from New York to act as shop superintendent and liaison man. As expenses rose, and with them a need for better accounting, Hughes established the **Hughes Aircraft Company** as a division of the Hughes Tool Company.

First Flight

The Racer was finished on 10 August 1935. After eighteen months of secrecy, Hughes was ready to unveil the airplane that the press was calling his "mystery ship." A week later, Howard called his troops together and announced that he was going to test the H-1 himself, much to the chagrin of Palmer and Robert C. Kuhn, Toolco's president, both of whom pleaded with Howard to let someone else make the first flight, which was considered far too dangerous for a man of Hughes's wealth and importance.

The Racer was trucked over to Mines Field and made ready for flight the next day. As the mechanics were readying the Racer, now designated the **Hughes H-1**, for flight, Odekirk helped Howard to slip into his flight coveralls and a beat-up leather flight helmet. He climbed into the cockpit, strapped himself in, checked the controls, started the engine, and took off over the Pacific. The apprehension as to Howard's safety was put to rest, but although the airplane handled well, problems with the variable pitch propeller limited the Racer's top speed to around 250 mph. Howard made several more flights in it until he was sure that all the "kinks" had been worked out.

By then, he had accumulated 2 hours and 20 minutes in the H-1, which was easily capable of speeds well in excess

Preparing the H-1 for its first flight. (Florida Air Museum)

"Ode" helping Howard into his flight gear. (Florida Air Museum)

of 300 mph. Jimmy Wedell's record of 305 mph had already been broken in France the year before by **Raymond Delmonte** in a **Caudron C-460** that had reportedly cost a million dollars to build and was constructed with the aid of the French Air Ministry. Hughes was convinced that he could easily surpass Delmonte's 314-mph mark.

Hughes H-1A Racer

In this book, the aircraft nomenculture has followed a convention that has customarily distinguished the two variants of the Hughes Racer. Both were H-1 Racers, with different wings, and other minor modifications. The transcontinental version is known as the H-1B (see page 35).

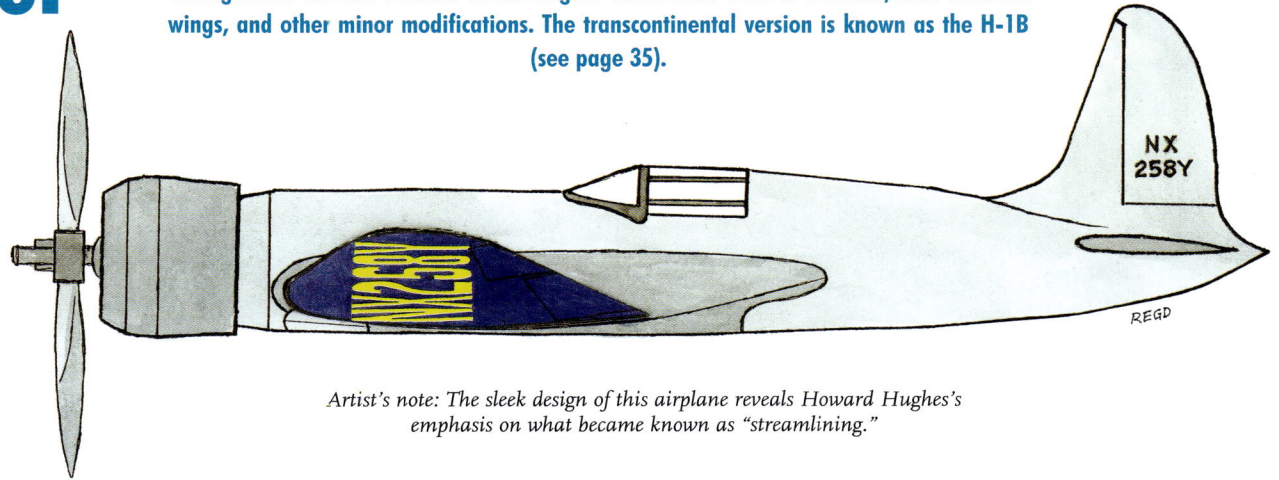

Dick Palmer's Design Detail

The Hughes H-1A Racer was designed with only a single objective: speed. It was the most advanced aircraft of its day and it incorporated all the latest improvements in aeronautical design and streamlining. The landing gear retracted hydraulically and was perfectly faired into the wing, which had gently curved fillets where it joined the fuselage. This reduced drag, stabilized the airflow, and prevented the potentially dangerous phenomena of eddying and tail buffeting. The fuselage was constructed of aluminum sheets that were butt-jointed together to form a smooth contour. The external surfaces were all flush-riveted and all fasteners and screw-heads were aligned with the projected airflow. The cockpit had an adjustable seat and featured a Plexiglas windscreen that slid forward on tracks to allow entry. During take off and landing, the side windows were lowered into the fuselage, the windscreen slid forward, and the seat raised for better visibility.

The one-piece wing was constructed of wood, with two main box spars and numerous supporting ribs. It was sheathed with oversized plywood that was closely shaped to produce the optimum airfoil shape before it was covered in cloth, painted, and waxed to an extremely high gloss. Wood was chosen, because there was nothing better suited to produce the exact contour shape of the airfoil. The control surfaces were made of aluminum, covered with fabric, and doped in a deep royal blue to match the blue paint of the wing. The rudder and elevators were similarly made of aluminum, covered with fabric, and doped to match the aluminum finish of the fuselage.

The Engine

Power was provided by a Pratt & Whitney SA1-G Twin Wasp Jr., rated at 700 hp, which was boosted to more than 900 hp through revised carburetor settings and the use of 100-octane fuel. The engine was covered with a close-fitting bell-shaped cowling to reduce aerodynamic drag and improve engine cooling. It was fitted with a two-bladed Hamilton Standard controllable pitch propeller with external counterweights.

Artist's note: The sleek design of this airplane reveals Howard Hughes's emphasis on what became known as "streamlining."

Length	27 ft
Wing Span	25 ft
Engine	Pratt & Whitney SA1-G (700 hp)
Seating	Pilot only
Cruise Speed	352 mph
MGTOW	5,492 lb.

Size comparison with Constellation (p.55)

The H-1 Racer was a one-of-a-kind airplane conceived and built by Howard Hughes in eighteen months at a cost of $105,000. It was the first high-speed monoplane that combined all the following aeronautical advances:

- **wind tunnel-tested streamlining**
- **flush riveting**
- **hydraulically-retractable landing gear**
- **low frontal area radial engine**
- **close fitting bell-shaped cowling to reduce drag**
- **variable pitch, constant speed propeller**
- **100-octane fuel**

World Landplane Speed Record, 1935

The First Attempt

Hughes made his first attempt at the landplane speed record on 12 September 1935 over a closed course, set up at the Martin airport in Santa Ana, California. He had the Racer's Twin Wasp Jr. tuned for maximum output, using the new 100-octane fuel that had been shipped in five-gallon containers from the Shell refinery in New Orleans. Howard arrived at the airfield late in the afternoon and was met by representatives of the National Aeronautics Association and the International Federation Aeronautique (F.A.I.). Howard took off in fading daylight and made four passes, setting an unofficial record of 352 mph. The second set of runs was disallowed because he had dived into the course. They would try again the next day, Friday the 13th.

The Record Attempt

Hughes had to make four passes between the electric-eye photo-timers, spaced 3 kilometers apart: two up-wind and two down wind. Reputable pilots Amelia Earhart and Paul Mantz were in the air to make sure that Howard not only stayed below 1,000 feet before the dive into the course, but also went no higher then 200 feet between the timers. He made the two sets of required runs and then added a third for insurance. He was going around to complete the fourth set, when the engine quit. To keep the weight down, the Racer had just enough high-octane gasoline for the standard set of tests. Howard had failed to watch his gas gauge.

The Crash Landing and a Record

He turned into the wind for landing, and began a normal gliding approach for the airfield. Without power, he was unable to get the landing gear down, and was about to undershoot the air strip when he made a near-perfect belly-landing in a beet field about one mile short of the airport. When the Racer disappeared from view, everyone on the field jumped into cars and headed for the crash site. They found Howard sitting on the cockpit, writing a report on the flight in a notebook.

The Racer sustained only minor damage, the officials considered the landing to be controlled; the timing results would stand: the Racer had been clocked at 352.388 mph, 40 mph faster than the previous record made in France.

Howard posing for the camera after setting the Racer down in a beet field.
(Florida Air Museum)

Howard inspecting the Racer after his forced landing.
(Author's collection)

Beechcraft A17F Staggerwing

The Airplane

The Beechcraft Model 17 was a "staggerwing" biplane with an enclosed four-seat cabin. It was so called because of the unusual arrangement of the wings in which the upper wing was set back from the lower wing, rather than the reverse, which was the conventional style. The prototype was introduced in 1932, with production beginning in 1934. During its lifetime, which continued until 1948, Beechcraft designed and built a total of 785 Staggerwings in four different variants, all with fixed landing gears, except the B17L.

Hughes's interest in the Staggerwing was typical of the man. The aircraft, of metal and fabric construction, was Walter Beech's first, and designed by Ted Wells. For its time, it could be described as a "hot ship". But it was not cheap, and was consequently popular only among business executives who could afford the high price during the Depression years. Towards the end of its production life, the landing gear dispensed with the spats and was fully retractable. Eventually it sold well.

The Hughes Variant

While the Racer was being assembled in the spring of 1935, Howard bought a Beechcraft A17F, powered by a big 9-cylinder 690 hp Wright engine. The airplane had a top speed of 235 mph, and although its flight characteristics were predictable, it was a "hot" ship that was tricky to land, a feature that led to its nickname the "Beast." Howard bought the airplane to sharpen his flying technique and to prepare himself for the Racers. He made many short flights in the Staggerwing, just to practice high speed takeoffs and landings under various conditions. In August 1935 he flew the airplane to Wright Aeronautical for an engine upgrade, leaving his mechanic, **Joe Herron**, to oversee the job of converting the R-1820-F11 to an R-1820-F56. The latter was a high-altitude Navy engine that was not available on the civilian market, but Hughes had the wherewithal — unspecified but effective — to get what he wanted. After the conversion, the engine's horsepower jumped from 690 to 745 hp. Although he flew the airplane after it was returned to the West Coast, most flights were short and, having served its purpose, it soon became a "hangar queen" until it was sold in August 1937.

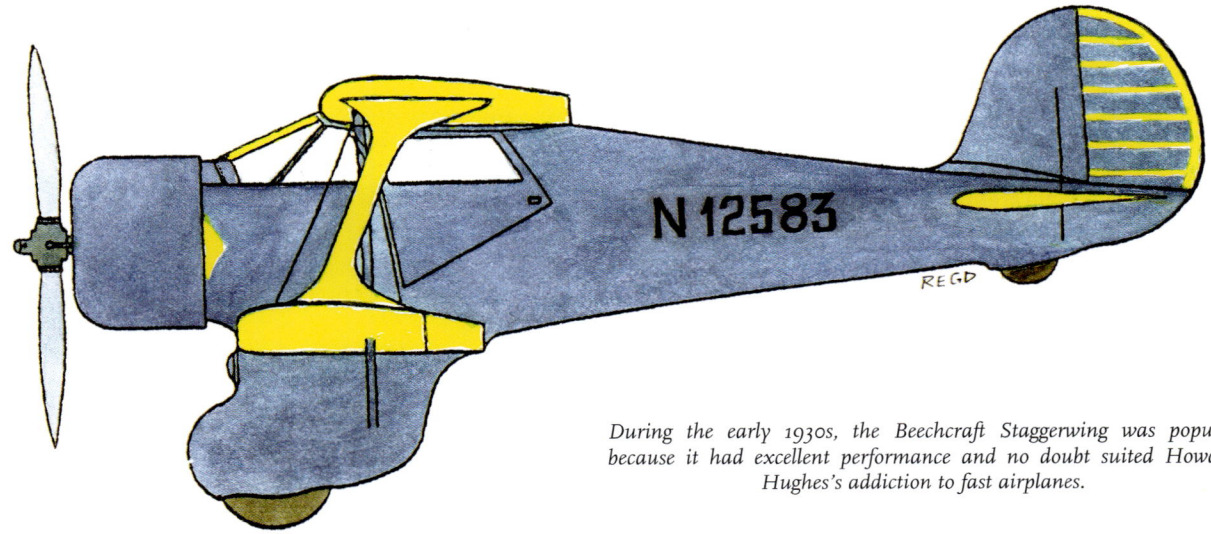

During the early 1930s, the Beechcraft Staggerwing was popular because it had excellent performance and no doubt suited Howard Hughes's addiction to fast airplanes.

Length	24 ft
Wing Span	35 ft
Engine	Wright R-1820 F11 (690 hp)
Seating	4 (including pilot)
Cruise Speed	212 mph
MGTOW	5,200 lb.
Normal Range	750 miles

Size comparison with Constellation (p.55)

Howard Hughes's Beechcraft A17F Staggerwing, a "hot ship," contrasted with his H-1 Racer and the Northrop Gamma which were even hotter "hot ships". His familiarity with a variety of aircraft confirmed his versatility, not only in his piloting expertise, but also in his knowledge of the structures and systems of all types of airplanes.

Transcontinental Speed Record, 1936

Speed vs. Range

After he had captured the world's speed record, Hughes began to think about flying the Racer to yet greater glory. The most tempting target was the United States transcontinental record that had recently been shattered by **Roscoe Turner**, who made the flight from the West Coast to the East Coast in 10 hours, 2 minutes, 57 seconds. Although the H-1 Racer could easily outpace Turner's airplane, it did not have the fuel capacity to fly across the country non-stop. Hughes put Palmer and Odekirk to work. Their assignment: to build a second, larger, set of wings for the Racer, so as to hold more fuel and to provide greater lift.

While they modified the Racer, Hughes spent much of his time in the air, jotting down observations on wind velocity, air speed, engine performance, and fuel consumption. Always an intense perfectionist, he was especially interested in high-altitude flying as a way to elude bad weather and to increase his speed — an idea he undoubtedly picked up from **William C. "Rocky" Rockefeller**, an expert in meteorology and aerodymanics from Cal-Tech, and whom he hired as a consultant.

Instrument Testing

As Howard accumulated more flight time at the higher altitudes, he began to question the accuracy of the airspeed indicators that he had been using. One day he set up an experiment to test this theory. On a map, he laid out a 72-mile course from Mount Wilson, north to Los Angeles, to San Jacinto Peak, and on to Palm Springs. Placing several of is employees at specified points along the route, Hughes flew over the course at 15,000 feet. Later, by comparing the readings on his airspeed indicator with the timing of the observers posted on land, Hughes proved that he had been right. He was traveling 15 miles faster than his instruments showed.

Practice Runs

For practice, Howard once again flew commercially, this time as a co-pilot for T.W.A. — presumably under his own name this time. It is likely that the arrangements were made through **Jack Frye**, a childhood friend who was then the airline's president. By December 1936 he had accumulated almost 34 hours flying time in Douglas DC-2s on scheduled runs throughout the eastern and mid-western states. On Christmas Eve of that year, Howard celebrated his 31st birthday by making practice landings in the DC-1, the prototype of the famous DC-2/DC-3 series, at the Kansas City Airport.

Coast-to-Coast

In January 1936, Hughes was back in California, waiting for the right weather conditions for his record-setting attempt. On the 13th, Howard was eating a late breakfast at 11:30 a.m. when he received word — probably from Rocky Rockefeller — that conditions were perfect across the entire country. Pushing back from the table, he rushed out to his car and headed for Burbank where the Northrop Gamma was sitting, fueled with 700 gallons of gas and ready for take-off. Grabbing only his leather helmet and goggles, he jumped into the cockpit and took off at 12:15 p.m., heading east.

Shortly after climbing over the San Gabriel Mountains, he ran into heavy overcast, then leveled off at 15,000 feet and tried to get radio bearings. But his antenna had been torn away during take-off, and he would be out of contact with the ground for the entire trip. After two hours of flying blind he came into the clear over Santa Fe. Watching his fuel consumption, he climbed to 18,000 feet where he could pick up more wind speed, allowing him to throttle back. North of Wichita, he ran into rough air. One gust buffeted the plane so strongly that it knocked the dash board compass needle off its point. Instead of hunting for his spare compass, Howard navigated by using the map on his lap, identifying the cities on his route by their lights.

Los Angeles-Newark

When he landed at Newark just after midnight at 12:42:10 a.m. the following morning, the only people on hand to meet him were the two F.A.I. timers who were there to authenticate the new record that he had just set. Howard Hughes had crossed the country in 9 hours, 27 minutes and 10 seconds, beating Roscoe's Turner's time by 35 minutes.

Later that day, newspapermen had to rouse Howard from his hotel room at the Waldorf-Astoria to obtain details of the flight. His success, he explained, was attributed to the Gamma and its new engine. "All I did was to sit there. The engine did all the work." It would not be long, he told them, before regular transport plans will make the Los Angeles-New York trip in 10 hours or less. He would fulfil this prophecy when, later, the Constellation (that he had a hand in designing) did so.

Jackie Cochran's Gamma.

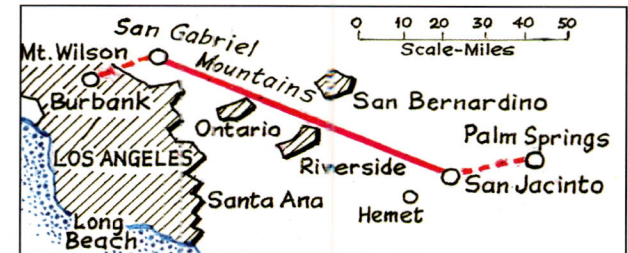

Hughes tested his airspeed indicators over this course.

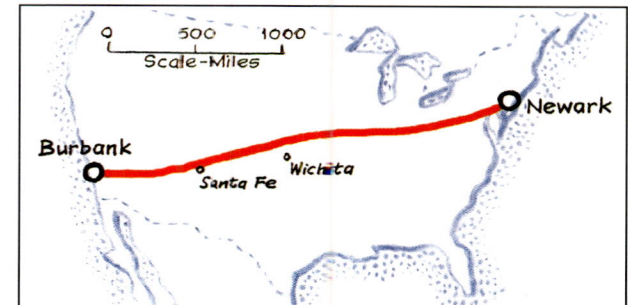

The weather was uncertain for most of the way across the country, and his instruments let him down, but Howard found his way, using a map.

Northrop Gamma 2G

The Gamma

The Gamma was introduced in 1933 by the newly-established Northrop Corporation of Inglewood, California. It was a low-wing all-metal cantilever monoplane with an enclosed cockpit set on top of the fuselage, aft of the wings.

The Gamma was the second in the series of all-metal airplanes designed by Jack Northrop. The first was the Alpha that Northrop had developed when he sold his research company to United Aircraft and Transportation in 1930. The Alpha carried passengers in an enclosed cabin, along with 465 pounds of mail. It was one of the first production aircraft with an all-metal structure, a semi-monocoque fuselage, and a cantilever stressed-skin wing.

Howard Modifies the Gamma

While the Racer was being modified, Howard continued to look for an airplane that was capable of operating efficiently in the upper atmosphere over the long distances that he could use to prepare himself for his record-breaking cross-country flight. He found the perfect airplane at Mines Field, the site which is not Los Angeles International Airport (LAX). The airplane was a **Northrop Gamma 2G** that **Jacqueline Cochran** had flown in her unsuccessful attempt to win that year's 135 Bendix Trophy Race. **Frank Hawks** had used an earlier model Gamma in his record setting transcontinental flight of 1933, but Cochran refused to sell her 2G Variant. In November, however, after weeks of Howard's incessant pestering, Jackie, who needed the cash, relented, and agreed to lease the Gamma.

Inevitable Hughes Modifications

Howard flew Jackie's Northrop Gamma to the Union Air Terminal in Burbank, where Hughes Aircraft personnel, now housed in their own hangar at one end of the field, immediately began to modify the airplane according to Hughes's demanding specifications. They added more fuel tanks, faired the tail wheel, reworked the cockpit, and installed a supercharged 9-cylinder Wright R-1820G Cyclone engine that was rated at 1,000 hp for take-off.

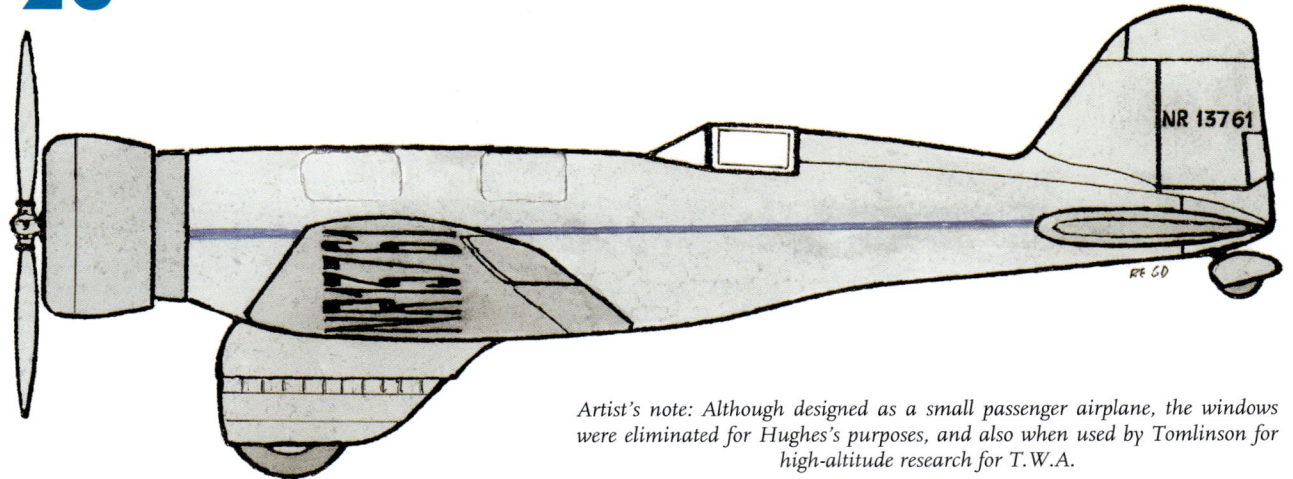

Artist's note: Although designed as a small passenger airplane, the windows were eliminated for Hughes's purposes, and also when used by Tomlinson for high-altitude research for T.W.A.

Length	30 ft
Wing Span	48 ft
Engine	Wright GR-1820-G (925 hp)
Seating	Pilot only
Cruise Speed	200+ mph
MGTOW	9,550 lb.

Size comparison with Constellation (p.55)

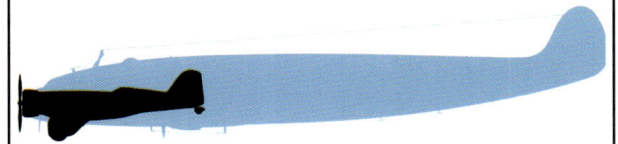

The Gamma at Floyd Bennett Field after Hughes's record-breaking run. During the early 1930s this airfield was used almost entirely by the military, and it was one of the earliest to have a concrete runway. The commercial airfield for New York was at Newark, where the runway area was of cinders, and sometimes unreliable during bad weather. In 1938, the German Fw 200 Condor landplane used Floyd Bennett Field's hard-surfaced runway for its landing on its pioneering non-stop Atlantic crossing from Berlin to New York.

Twelve Great Months, 1936–37

Miami-New York

Howard left the Gamma at Newark and returned to the West Coast on a commercial airliner. He kept busy in Southern California until the end of March 1936 when he took another airline ride back to Newark. After checking out the Gamma, he flew it to Miami to visit Gloria Baker. On 21 April, Howard took off from the Pan American Airport, climbed to 13,750 feet (he had forgotten to turn on his oxygen tank before taking off) and headed for Floyd Bennett Field in New York. He made the trip in 4 hours 21 minutes and 32 seconds — 39 minutes faster than the previous record set by Jimmy Wedell in July 1933.

Chicago-Los Angeles

On 13 May, Howard took off once again in the Gamma for the return trip to California. His flight back started out in a very leisurely fashion, making a stop in Chicago, to take care of the Toolco interests that gave him the money that kept him up in the sky. Next day, in Chicago, a friend bet him $50 that he could not have lunch in Chicago and dinner in California. He took the bet. He roared into Glendale Airport at 7:15 p.m. — after a record 8 hours, 10 minutes and 25 seconds of flying — and in time for dinner.

"I learned more things in that eight hours than in the last fifteen years," he laughed as he ate the 75-cent roast beef dinner that had cost him $500 to be in time for. "And it was the narrowest escape I ever had. The only thing that worked on my ship was the engine… A couple of hours out, everything went haywire. The air-speed indicator suddenly dropped to zero. Then the oxygen tank connections fouled. Finally, when I thought my troubles were over and California was in sight, my oil pressure went down to nothing. I started pumping by hand."

Coast-to-Coast-Again

The long-wing transcontinental H-1B, that Howard was now calling the "Winged Bullet," was ready at the end of December 1936. He made test flights in the new ship three days after Christmas and again on 17 January 1937. The next day, a favorable weather report at midnight caused an unexpected shift in his plans. He had run fuel-consumption

tests on the H-1B during the day, and had planned to defer the transcontinental flight until later in the week, when the news of favorable winds caused him to start on only two hours notice. His abrupt departure was a calculated decision to thwart Jimmy Wedell, who was planning his own attempt at the record.

At 2:14 in the morning of 20 January and pitch dark, Howard rolled down the runway and took off from the Union Air Terminal in Burbank. As in 1936, he ran into unfavorable weather conditions from the start. Climbing to 15,000 feet, he leveled off above the clouds and throttled back, only to find that the conditions were still choppy and rough. Adjusting his new oxygen mask, he added power and climbed to 20,000 feet. An hour and a half later, he began to have trouble breathing through the rubber nosepiece and his hands and legs began to feel numb. He nosed the ship down to 15,000 feet and tore the rubber gadget from his face, gradually regaining full consciousness. Once again his radio failed as did the cockpit heater, but the strong tail winds that he picked up eliminated tentative plans to stop in Chicago for fuel. He arrived ahead of schedule when he streaked over Newark Airport just after noon at 12:42 p.m. — only 9.42 a.m. at Burbank. When he stepped out of the aircraft, he was greeted by Dick Palmer, Al Lodwick of the Curtiss-Wright Company, and Bill Zint, the official timer. He had set a new coast-to-coast record of 7 hours, 28 minutes, and 25 seconds.

Howard Hughes, debonair and self-assured — as he had every right to be — after breaking the transcontinental speed record in the Northrop Gamma. The flight had not been easy, as his oxygen mask, his radio, and his cockpit heater, had all failed. Hughes's airmanship often seemed to be contradictory. At times he would take unnecessary risks, while at other times, as on this occasion, he would be quite resourceful. As the two pictures on this page suggest, he seldom displayed any extremes of emotion. (Lakeland Library)

Howard Hughes pictured beside his "crack air speedster" before roaring westward to Los Angeles in an effort to set a "lunch-to-dinner" record. (Library of Congress)

National Recognition

The Harmon Trophy

The Harmon Trophy had been established in 1926 by Clifford B. Harmon, a wealthy sportsman and pioneering aviator, who flew across Long Island Sound in 1910 in an airplane constructed of bamboo and piano wire. The Trophy is now awarded annually to the world's outstanding aviator. In Hughes's time, the recipient was determined by the International League of Aviators, who awarded the Trophy to the individual who, in the previous year, had contributed most to aviation.

Howard Meets the President

Howard was nominated for the 1936 award for the records that he had established, and for his outstanding contributions to aeronautics. The award was presented by President Roosevelt at the White House Oval Office on 2 March 1937 (see p.34). Thanking the President, Howard explained that he

"was deeply interested in seeing that aviation goes ahead, not only from a speed standpoint, but likewise from a safety standpoint, and I assure you that in the future, as in the past, I will devote my efforts unselfishly to the progress of this new form of transportation."

Hughes's Cross Country Flight Records

Route	Aircraft	Date	Flying Time
Los Angeles–Newark	Northrop Gamma	14 January 1936	9 hr 27 min 10 sec
Miami–New York	Northrop Gamma	21 April 1936	4 hr 21 min 32 sec
Chicago–Los Angeles	Northrop Gamma	14 May 1936	8 hr 10 min 25 sec
Los Angeles–Newark	Hughes H-1B	20 January 1937	7 hr 28 min 25 sec

The moment of triumph and national hero status.

Al Lodwick greets Howard Hughes upon his arrival at Newark Airport. (Florida Air Museum)

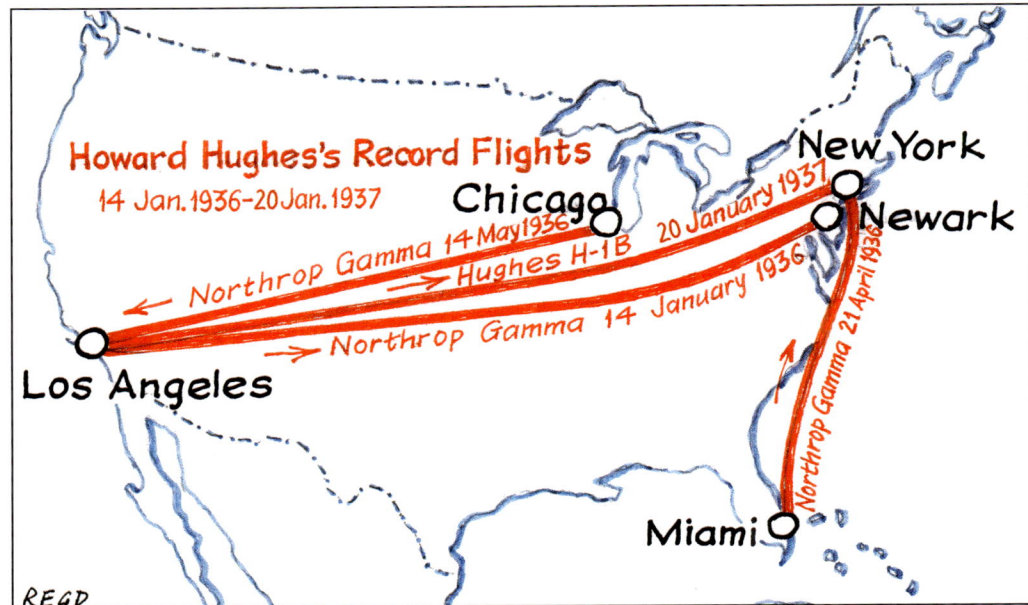

Howard Hughes's Record Flights
14 Jan. 1936–20 Jan. 1937

New York · Newark · Chicago · Los Angeles · Miami

Northrop Gamma 14 May 1936
Hughes H-1B 20 January 1937
Northrop Gamma 14 January 1936
Northrop Gamma 21 April 1936

REGD

The Harmon Trophy

An Outstanding Airman

In today's aviation world, during which airplanes are as familiar to the general public as motor cars, radio, and television, outstanding aeronautical events receive scant attention except, regrettably, only where violence or tragedy are involved. But during the two decades of the interwar period, the pace of technological advances in aeronautics was such that, every year, special achievements, including record-breaking events, were headline news.

In Europe, the emphasis was on speed, with sucessive records invariably achieved in races that had been sponsored by Henri Schneider, a French arms manufacturer, who created the annual Schneider Trophy races. In the United States, which did not then enjoy the universal dominance that was to haven in post-war years, speed was not the aramount criterion of excellence, and various trophies were awarded on a wider basis, involving mainly distance and endurance.

The Harmon International Trophy

The most prestigous of these, the Harmon International Trophy, consisted of three categories, aviator, aviatrix, and aeronaut (or airmen, airwomen, and balloonists, respectively). Among the airmen, until 1935, seven of the ten awards since the inception of the Trophy in 1926 had been for non-U.S. aviators. The three Americans were Charles Lindbergh, for his spectacular New York-Paris non-stop flight in 1927, Wiley Post's round-the-world epic in 1933, and Pan American's Capt. Ed Musick, for inaugurating the world's first trans-oceanic air service in 1935.

Howard Hughes joined this élite company in 1936, when, among other flights, he beat the transcontinental speed record across the U.S.A. After a brief interlude in 1937, when Dick Merrill made the first commercial trans-Atlantic airplane flight, carrying a film of the coronation of King George VI he did it again. He was the only American airman to have won the Harmon International Trophy twice—within three years—during a period when, all over the world, aviators were still seeking fame and fortune. Of course, Howard did not have to worry about the fortune.

THE HARMON INTERNATIONAL AVIATOR TROPHY WINNERS 1926–1939

Year	Winner	Nationality
1926	Lt. Col. George Pelletier-Doisy	French
1927	Charles Lindbergh	U.S.
1928	Col. Arturo Ferrario	Italian
1929	Maj. Dieudonné Costes	French
1930	Maj. Dieudonné Costes	French
1931	Air Marshall Italo Balbo	Italian
1932	Wolfgang von Gronau	German
1933	Wiley Post	U.S.
1934	Charles W. A. Scott	British
1935	Capt. Ed Musick	U.S.
1936	Howard Hughes	U.S.
1937	Henry T. Merrill	U.S.
1938	Howard Hughes	U.S.
1939	Maj. Alexander P. de Seversky	U.S.

Postcript

Awards for the Harmon Trophies were suspended during the Second World War. General Jimmy Doolittle was awarded it for distinguished work, 1940–49; together with Geoffrey de Havilland (posthumously) chief test pilot of the British firm, and Capt. "Chuck" Yeager, first pilot to fly supersonically, both with honorable mentions. Subsequently, with opportunities for record-breaking fast diminishing, the prestige of winning the Harmon Trophy also diminished. Howard Hughes's achievement in winning it twice, during an era when it epitomized the achievement, was unique in America.

The Harmon International Aviator Trophy is now preserved by the National Air and Space Museum of the Smithsonian Institution in Washington, D.C.

Presidential Roosevelt awarding the Harmon Trophy in 1936. (Florida Air Museum)

Hughes H-1B Racer

Modifying the Racer

Changes were made in the H-1A Racer to prepare it for Howard's record-setting transcontinental flight. New wings were added with greater span, greater area, and a different airfoil shape that incorporated larger fuel tanks. The cockpit was changed, additional navigational aids and a radio were added, and an oxygen system (an innovation still in the experimental stage at the time) installed. The engine was replaced by a different Twin Wasp Jr., taken from Jackie Cochran's Northrop Gamma for increased durability and power. Nominally rated at 700 hp, Hughes's crew found ways to boost it to 850 hp for the long haul, and near 1,000 hp for short periods.

A New World to Conquer

Howard Hughes might have declared, after this year of remarkable success, "you ain't seen nothin' yet." With world speed and U.S. transcontinental range records, plus a prestigious national trophy, behind him, he stepped up his own self-imposed level of ambition. With his deep pockets to finance any project, he now, in 1936, as this telegram to Wright Field shows, aimed to stretch his own spirits and stamina to their limits, and switched to another airplane.

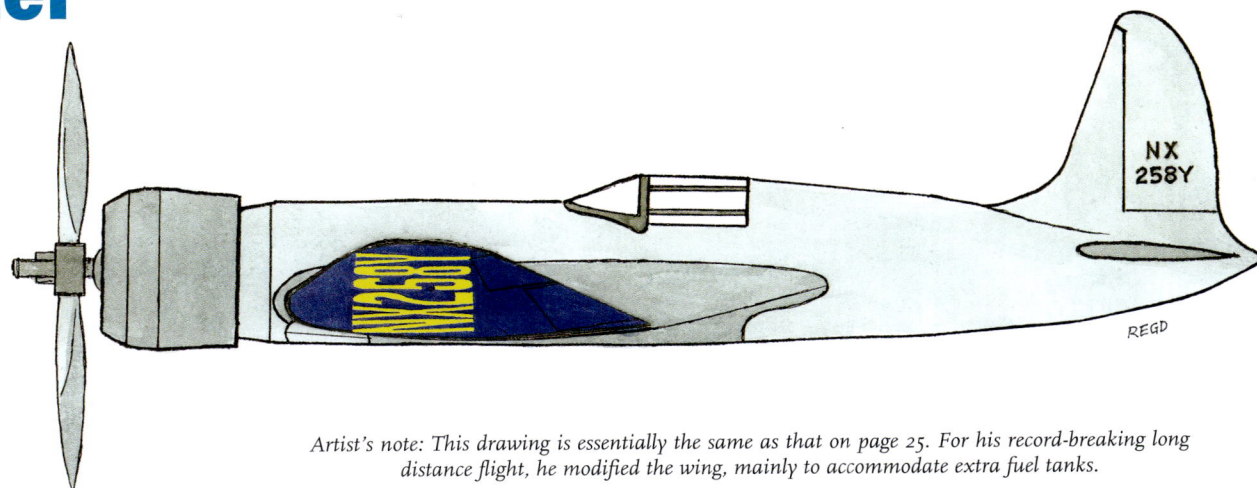

Artist's note: This drawing is essentially the same as that on page 25. For his record-breaking long distance flight, he modified the wing, mainly to accommodate extra fuel tanks.

Length	27 ft
Wing Span	32 ft
Engine	Pratt & Whitney SA5-G (850 hp)
Seating	Pilot only
Cruise Speed	300+ mph
MGTOW	5,492 lb.

Size comparison with Constellation (p.55)

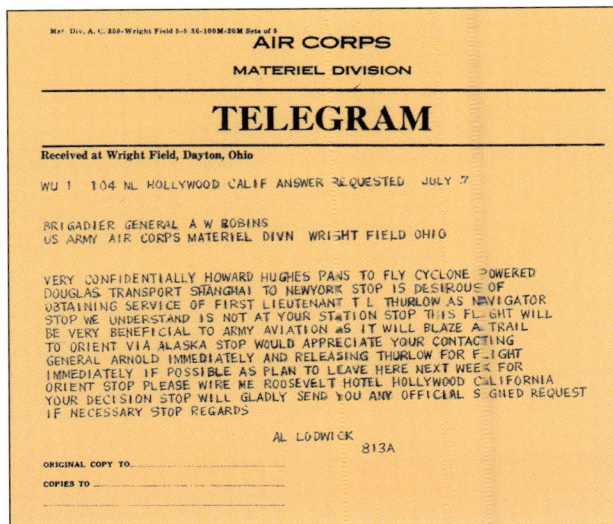

(Left) The telegram shows that Howard valued good navigation and set out to hire an excellent navigator. Coincidentally he had a good relationship with the Army.

Mat Div. A. C. 369-Wright Field 5-5 35-100M-20M Sets of 5

AIR CORPS

MATERIEL DIVISION

TELEGRAM

Received at Wright Field, Dayton, Ohio

WU 1 104 NL HOLLYWOOD CALIF ANSWER REQUESTED JULY 7

BRIGADIER GENERAL A W ROBINS
US ARMY AIR CORPS MATERIEL DIVN WRIGHT FIELD OHIO

VERY CONFIDENTIALLY HOWARD HUGHES PLANS TO FLY CYCLONE POWERED
DOUGLAS TRANSPORT SHANGHAI TO NEWYORK STOP IS DESIROUS OF
OBTAINING SERVICE OF FIRST LIEUTENANT T L THURLOW AS NAVIGATOR
STOP WE UNDERSTAND IS NOT AT YOUR STATION STOP THIS FLIGHT WILL
BE VERY BENEFICIAL TO ARMY AVIATION AS IT WILL BLAZE A TRAIL
TO ORIENT VIA ALASKA STOP WOULD APPRECIATE YOUR CONTACTING
GENERAL ARNOLD IMMEDIATELY AND RELEASING THURLOW FOR FLIGHT
IMMEDIATELY IF POSSIBLE AS PLAN TO LEAVE HERE NEXT WEEK FOR
ORIENT STOP PLEASE WIRE ME ROOSEVELT HOTEL HOLLYWOOD CALIFORNIA
YOUR DECISION STOP WILL GLADLY SEND YOU ANY OFFICIAL SIGNED REQUEST
IF NECESSARY STOP REGARDS

AL LODWICK
813A

ORIGINAL COPY TO

COPIES TO

(Right) The Hughes H-1B, a superb design, born of Howard's demanding standards that emphasized smooth surfaces for minimum aerodynamics drag, together with Dick Palmer's design engineering.

The Modern Airliner

Boeing v. Douglas

When the **DC-1 (Douglas Commercial No. 1)** first took to the air on 1 July 1933, it represented a technological breakthrough. Its superiority over the Boeing 247 would lead to the development of the Douglas DC-2 and DC-3 airliners that would dominate the world of air transport not only in the U.S.A., but in Europe, Australia, China, and Japan, for the remainder of the decade. It was born as the direct result of T.W.A.'s frustration with Boeing, which refused to deliver Boeing 247s until it had completed an order for the rival United Aircraft and Transport Corporation group, which included Boeing Air Transport, later to merge to form United Air Lines. T.W.A.'s president, **Jack Frye,** wrote a letter to five other manufacturers, with specifications for an airliner that would be superior to the Boeing product. Tested by no less than Charles Lindbergh, who was T.W.A.'s technical consultant, the DC-1 won the competition.

Howard Puts the DC-1 to Use

Designed as a technology demonstrator, the one-and-only DC-1 was originally powered by two 690 hp Wright SGR-1820F radial engines. It operated briefly in service before Transcontinental added more powerful engines and modified the airplane for use as a flying laboratory to investigate high altitude flight conditions. The fuselage of this airplane was filled with 9 additional 180-gallon fuel tanks and two more oil tanks, for a total oil capacity of 135-gallons. T.W.A. used the DC-1 to establish a number of world records for load-carrying, distance, and speed over a triangular course (the longest duration was 19 hours made by Tommy Tomlinson and Joe Bartles) before it was purchased by Hughes Tool Company on 30 January 1936.

With its extra fuel tanks installed, the DC-1 had a range of approximately 5,000 miles making it a natural candidate for Howard's future plans for even longer flights around the globe. He took delivery of the DC-1 in Kansas City on 1 February 1936 and shot eight landings before proceeding to New York. Four days latter he flew the DC-1 to United Airport in Burbank, with a stop at Wichita — 16 hours, 30 minutes. After a few local test flights, Howard had the aircraft overhauled and had more powerful engines installed.

For his own purposes, to accomodate extra fuel tanks, plus other installations for its role as a Flying Laboratory, Howard's DC-1 had no windows — they had been blocked out, possibly because of his obsession with aerodynamics perfection.

Trans-Pacific Plan

In the spring of 1936, Hughes began to formulate plans to fly the Douglas transport from Shanghai to New York. Such a flight would benefit aviation by blazing a new air route to the Orient by way of Alaska. On 7 July 1936, **Al Lodwick** — the coordinator and manager of Hughes long distance flights — sent a telegram (see previous page) on Hughes's behalf to General A. W. Robins, Chief of the Air Corps Material Command at Wright Field, to ask if Lieutenant Thomas Thurlow could be released in time to act as navigator for the flight, which was scheduled to begin the following week. Thurlow, who had just reported to Wright Field, could not be spared and the flight never took place. Instead, Howard changed his plans — dramatically. He intended to fly around the world.

In mid-August, Howard flew the DC-1 across the country to test the newly-installed Sperry automatic gyro pilot. Accompanying him were key members of the support team that he had assembled for his round-the-world flight: **Dick Stoddart**, radio operator; **Harry Connor**, navigator; **Edward Lund**, mechanic, **"Rocky" Rockefeller**, meteorologist, and the experienced Al Lodwick, operations manager. The DC-1 *Flying Laboratory* landed at Floyd Bennett Field at 10:20 a.m. on 11 August, having stopped overnight at Wright Field in Dayton so that Howard could meet with General Robins.

The "Flying Laboratory" after landing at Floyd Bennett field on 11 August 1936 having completed a flight from Dayton, Ohio in less than three and a half-hours. Hughes was testing a new type of radio direction finder — the antenna for which can bee seen here at the top of the fuselage — as a prelude to his round-the-world-flight. (Author's collection)

Note: Howard appears to be the man sitting in the cockpit. The man at the side door was probably Ed Lund, who, at the time, was Hughes's flight engineer.

Douglas DC-1

X223Y

TWA
TWA
U.S.MAIL A.M.34
MM/REGD

Artist's note: The vertical stabilizer and rudder on the DC-1 prototype were modified later to be standardized with the production DC-2s, and used intermittently on the T.W.A. routes.

T.W.A. Transport Version

Length	. . . . .60 ft
Wing Span	. . . . .85 ft
Engine	. . . . Wright SGR-1820F (690 hp) x 2 F-52 (850 hp) x 2
Seating	. . . . .Crew 2, Passengers 12
Cruise Speed	. . . . .165 mph
MGTOW	. . . . .17,500 lb.
Range	. . . . .1,000 miles

Configured for World Flight

Length	. . . . .60 ft
Wing Span	. . . . .85 ft
Engine	. . . . .Wright SGR-1820F-52 (850 hp) x 2
Seating	. . . . Crew 5
Cruise Speed	. . . . 170 mph (est.)
MGTOW	. . . . .24,000 lb.
Range	. . . . 4,000–5,000 miles

Size comparison with Constellation (p.55)

THE DOUGLAS TWINS COMPARED

	Length	Wing Span	MGTOW	Passengers
DC-1	60 ft	85 ft	17,500 lb.	12
DC-2	63 ft	85 ft	18,560 lb.	14
DC-3	64ft	95 ft	30,000 lb.	21

Note: After the Second World War, the DC-3 seating was invariably increased to 28 — seven rows of four seats abreast instead of three.

The DC-1 had quite a career, apart from being the original prototype for the famous Douglas commercial airliner series. After previous generations of passenger transport aircraft, this was the first in the United States to offer the kind of comfort that we enjoy today.

After Howard Hughes and T.W.A. no longer needed it, the DC-1 was shipped off to Spain, to serve on the Republican side, and was eventually written off there.

The unique DC-1 that was used by Hughes for practice take-offs and landings on Christmas Eve 1935. This picture was taken at the Grand Central Air Terminal at Glendale, not far from Burbank.

Howard's Next Flying Boat

Atlantic Problem

In the months that followed, Howard recognized the severe operational demands on any aircraft that had to cross the ocean, and decided to replace the DC-1 with a Sikorsky S-43 amphibian. As both aircraft had similar cruising speeds, the decision to use the S-43 appears to have been based mainly on safety. In the event of engine trouble or an emergency situation during an Atlantic — or any ocean — crossing, it would be possible to make a water landing _ albeit a hazardous one — with the amphibian. But if they were flying the DC-1, the crew would have to ditch the aircraft — always a dangerous operation in the North Atlantic Ocean, even during the summer, and even if the Pacific Ocean lived up to its name.

Howard's S-43 Variant

An order for Howard's S-43 was placed on 15 March 1937. The purchase price of $129,350 included the installation in the hull of four extra gasoline tanks that added 1,500 gallons of fuel to the 600 gallons carried in the wings. Other modifications and equipment, including a 130-gallon auxiliary oil tank, were also specified by Hughes, who was never satisfied with the standard features normally supplied by an aircraft's manufacturer.

To supervise construction, Howard sent Dick Palmer to the Sikorsky plane manufacturer in Stratford, Connecticut. As chief engineer of Hughes Aircraft, Palmer had the unenviable task of overseeing the countless details that Howard insisted on designing himself.

The Flying Boat Era

During the 1930s, the case for flying boats for long-distance airline operations was strong, simply because, in the event of a forced landing at sea, the aircraft was built like a boat, and was presumed to be able to float long enough for rescuers to arrive. Most of the intercontinental airlines used them: Pan American Airways, Britain's Imperial Airways, Air France, and Germany's Deutsche Lufthansa. Belgium and the Netherlands were exceptions, the former because its SABENA route to the Belgian Congo was almost entirely over land, the latter because K.L.M. always believed in landplanes for its overland route to the Dutch East Indies.

The 1938 Wake-up Call

Due warning was given to the flying boat adherents when, in 1938, the German Focke-Wulf Fw 200 Condor four-engined landplane flew non-stop from Berlin to New York and a few days later back to Berlin again. Air France was already flying the Farman 2200 landplanes across the South Atlantic.

When the Second World War ended, Douglas's DC-4s and Lockheed's Constellations (the latter with Howard Hughes's contribution, support, and indirect financing) rapidly replaced all the flying boats, which were soon scrapped or consigned to museums.

The wording of this telegram, by Howard Hughes himself, reveals the meticulous details of the preparations that he made for an important flight, and to which he gave his own intensely personal attention. The date of the telegram is sadly significant. Amelia Earhart and her navigator, Fred Noonan, lost their lives, while attempting to fly across the Pacific Ocean in a landplane, the Lockheed L-10. This aircraft could not float for very long and one theory is that the force of landing in the water knocked out the two flyers. Hughes was leaving no stone (or projection in the cockpit) unturned.

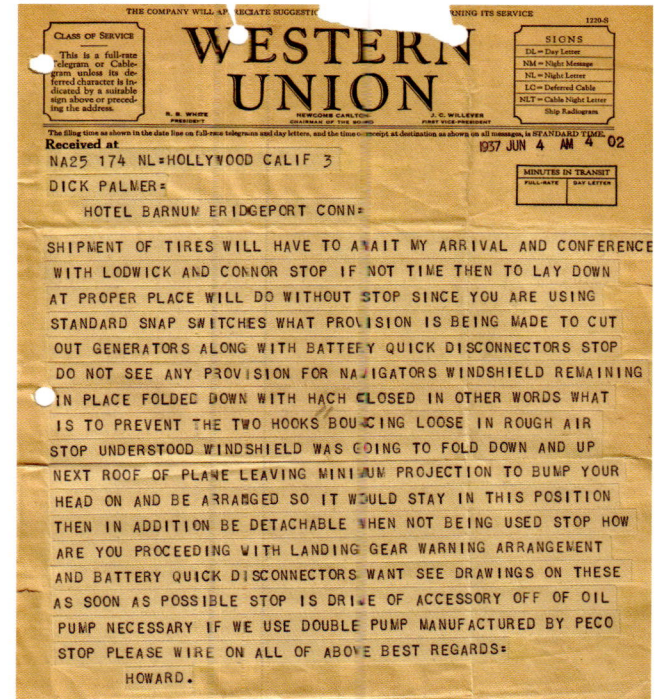

Howard Hughes's S-43 at Burbank

Sikorsky S-43

Baby Clipper

In 1934, Pan American Airways's founder and president, Juan T. Trippe, commissioned Igor Sikorsky to design an 18-passenger, twin-engined amphibian for coastal routes in the Caribbean and Central and South America. Sikorsky responded with the S-43, introduced in June 1935. It was equipped with two 750 hp engines, had a top speed of 190 mph, and a range 775 miles. In 1936 a Sikorsky S-43 set four payload-to-height records, reaching a maximum altitude of 29,950 feet.

The S-43s were often referred to as "Baby Clippers" in deference to their larger cousins, the Sikorsky S-40 and S-43 "Clippers," the first of which had entered service with Pan American Airways in November 1931. Trippe named these big flying boats "Clippers" because he felt that their role in expanding commerce was comparable to that of the Nineteenth Century "Clipper" ships that sailed across the Pacific.

The Big Sikorskys

Interestingly, Howard Hughes did not show great interest in the one airplane which, at the time, in the mid-1930s, was the only one that could fly across the world's oceans with some degree of reliability. In 1935, the long-range version of the S-42, the S-42B, was used for Pan American's survey flights across the Pacific Ocean, but were not used for passenger service because of the range limitations with a full payload of people and fuel on the 2,400-mile segment between San Francisco and Hawaii. This, incidentally, except for Easter Island-Tahiti in the southern Pacific, is the longest non-alternate route in the world. Even the larger Martin 130 "China Clippers" sometimes had to turn back at the halfway point.

Pan American also used the S-42B for the experimental survey flights across the Atlantic in 1937, but Howard had to choose the landplane solution because he could not obtain approval for the S-43, which appeared to be accident prone. Who knows, his reasoning may have been that he had to emulate, if not surpass, Juan Trippe, whom he could have regarded as rival.

Several millionaires ordered S-43s for their personal use. These were fitted out luxuriously, and used as "Flying Yachts."

Artist's Note: The Sikorsky S-43 was a true amphibian, in that its wheels could be fully retracted for conversion as a flying boat.

Length	51 ft
Wing Span	86 ft
Engine	Pratt & Whitney (750 hp) x 2
Seating	18
Cruise Speed	150 mph
MGTOW	29,500 lb.

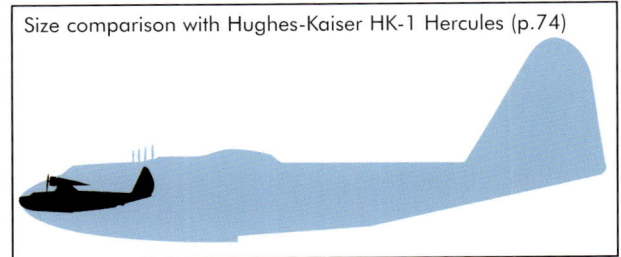

Size comparison with Hughes-Kaiser HK-1 Hercules (p.74)

To prepare his S-43 for the round-the-world flight, Howard had extra fuel tanks installed in the fuselage, equipped it with more powerful larger engines, and added extra special radio and navigation gear. Despite these modifications the Sikorsky became another of his "hangar queens" after he decided to shift to the much faster Lockheed 14.

Hughes's Sikorsky S-43. (Florida Air Museum)

Round-the-World Ambition

The Choice

During the summer of 1937, Howard Hughes quietly applied to the Bureau of Air Commerce in Washington, D.C. for permission to circumnavigate the globe. Not convinced that there was any scientific merit in such a flight, the Bureau turned him down. Characteristically, he was not easily dissuaded, and with the help of **Al Lodwick**, continued to pester the Bureau for the needed approvals. While he was waiting, Howard — he who was always current on the latest aircraft developments — became interested in a new transport airplane, the Model 14 Super Electra that had just been introduced by Lockheed Aircraft. Unlike the Douglas DC-1, which was a prototype, the Model 14 was an improved version of the highly successful Lockheed Model 10 Electra, which was smaller but faster than the DC-1.

Howard flew the Super Electra for the first time on 16 October 1937. Although it was a landplane, its high cruising speed made it an attractive alternative to the S-43 flying boat, which had been delivered just two weeks earlier. As his engineers began to prepare the S-43 for the world flight,

Noah Dietrich, Howard's business manager, placed an order for one of the Lockheed 14s on behalf of the Hughes Aircraft Company. Excluded from the contract price of $61,488 was the cost of the engines, propellers, and interior cabin, which was omitted from the order.

Global Preparation

The Hughes staff continued to prepare the S-43 for the world flight until the end of May 1938, when the Bureau of Air Commerce declined to approve the Sikorsky after an unexplained crash of another S-43 created concerns over its safety. Lodwick quickly dashed off a letter to Bureau requesting approval — which this time was forthcoming — to substitute the Model 14 for the flight that was now planned for the early part of July, when weather conditions would be ideal. The effort now shifted to the Lockheed 14, which had been delivered to the Hughes Aircraft hangar at Burbank's United Airport on 2 April 1938. With the scheduled time of the flight fast approaching, Howard began to devote a great deal of time to the project. He usually arrived around noon,

spent the entire afternoon working on the airplane, and continued long into the night, taking care of the many details that were associated with the forthcoming flight.

Howard prepares himself, complete with lucky hat, for flight in the Lockheed. (Lakeland Library)

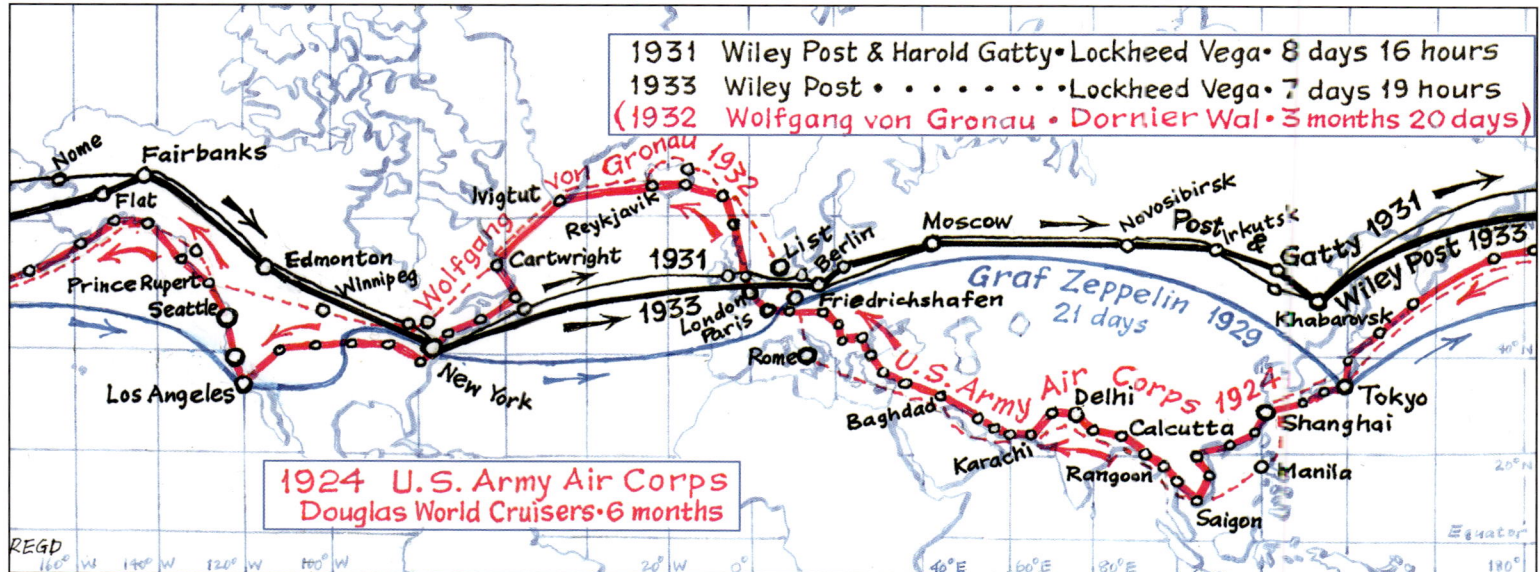

This map shows Wiley Post's achievements in perspective. He not only beat all previous records; he did so by a substantial margin, and in 1933, he did it alone. And he only had one good eye.

Lockheed 14

The Super Electra

The Super Electra was designed by a team of Lockheed engineers, headed by Hall Hibbard and Clarence "Kelly" Johnson, to supplement or supplant the new Douglas DC-3 commercial transport. Like the Model 10 and 12 Electras that preceded it, the Model 14 was an all-metal, twin-engined, twin-tail monoplane with a retractable main landing gear and fixed tail wheel. It was the first production aircraft to have Fowler flaps to reduce landing speeds and take-off distance. Construction of the first aircraft began in 1937. It was flown for the first time on 29 July 1937 of that year.

The Lockheed Twins

The Electra was faster than the Douglas DC-2 or DC-3, but could carry fewer passengers. Except on routes of limited traffic potential, it was able to earn less revenue than the well-established Douglases. The introduction into service of the Super Electras was also marred by several crashes.

The ultimate development of the series, however, the Lodestar, was used extensively during the Second World War, especially in Africa, and the Electras are remembered also by the pre-war British Airways, which promoted its speed against the slower competition from Imperial Airways and foreign airlines. It gained some publicity in Britain when it was selected to carry Prime Minister Neville Chamberlain to the ill-fated meeting with Adolf Hitler in 1938.

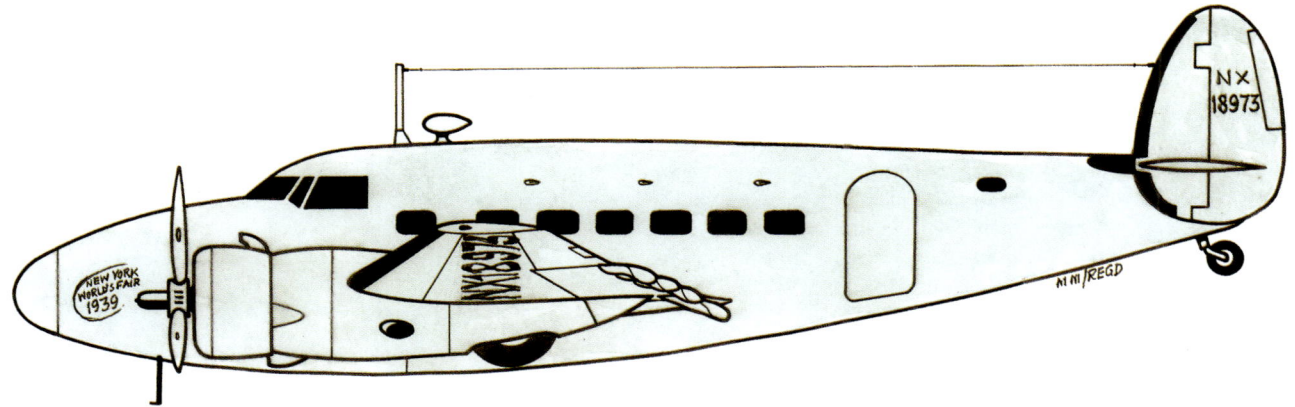

Artist's note: The series of Lockheed twin-engined airliners aimed to compete with the well established Douglas DC-2/DC-3 twins. Their 10-14-seat layouts were smaller than those of the Douglas 14-21-seaters but the Lockheeds were much faster.

Length	44 ft
Wing Span	65 ft
Engine	Wright R-1820 (900 hp) x 2
Seating	12
Cruise Speed	230 mph
MGTOW	20,000 lb.
Range	2,160 miles

Size comparison with Constellation (p.55)

LOCKHEED TRANSPORTS 1934–1940

	10 Electra	12 "Baby Electra"	14 "Super Electra"	Hughes's 14	18 Lodestar
Length (ft)	39	44	44	44	50
Wing Span (ft)	55	50	66	66	66
Engines	2	2	2	2	2
Takeoff power (ehp)	450	400	900	1,100	1,000
Seating	10	8	12	5 (crew)	17
Cruise Speed (mph)	185	212	230	230 (est)	229
Range (miles)	500	824	2,160	4,700	1,800
MGTOW (lb)	10,500	8,650	20,000	25,000	18,500

Note: Lockheed did not apply the L- prefix to its Model numbers.

The Lockheed 14 was the flagship of the pre-war British Airways, which put it into service in 1938.

Global Trail-Blazers

In 1931, **Wiley Post** and **Harold Gatty** had electrified America by circling the globe in 8 1/2 days. Two years later, Post became the first pilot to fly around the world alone when he flew the same route, and cut a day off the previous record. Both flights were completed in the *Winnie Mae*, a Lockheed Vega named for the daughter of its original owner, F. C. Hall, who hired Post to pilot the airplane, which had been purchased in June 1930.

Post's solo flight around the world in the *Winnie Mae* had greatly impressed Howard, who called it "one of the most remarkable feats of all time." Like Post, Hughes was fascinated by the scientific challenges of long-distance flight. He began to make plans for his own record-setting flight to circumnavigate the world in 1936.

Notable Precedents

To fly around the world had always been the ultimate goal of all pilots. It was a journey that demanded more than flying and navigation skills. Negotiations with foreign countries for overflying permission had to be obtained. Refuelling supplies and possible maintenance and spare parts servicing were necessary. Above all, no such 20,000–25,000-mile-flight could be undertaken without an expensive airplane and enough capital to sustain the operation.

In 1924, the U.S. Army Air Corps sponsored a truly historic event when four Douglas Cloudsters set off from California and after eight months, two of them completed the journey. In 1929 the German dirigible airship, the **Graf Zeppelin**, with its great lighter-than-air long range, circled the globe with only three stops. The German pilot, Wolfgang von Gronau flew around the world in 1932 in a Dornier Wal flying boat. Other long-distance flights were made across oceans but diplomatic problems with the Soviet Union was also a deterrent to the ultimate circumnavigation of the globe.

Tragically, Amelia Earhart, with her navigator, Fred Noonan, made the attempt in July 1937, via the mid-Pacific Ocean, but failed in the attempt. Howard Hughes had to meet an impressive challenge. He realized that Amelia's tragedy was caused by navigator Fred Noonan's almost impossible task of locating an island that was only a third of the size of New York's Central Park. Siberia was bigger.

Before his death in a plane crash in 1935, Post became one of the best-known fliers in the world, mainly because of a flight around the world with navigator Harold Gatty in 1931 and a similar solo flight in 1933. In addition, he was known for his pioneer work in high altitude flight and development of one of the first pressurized flight suits.

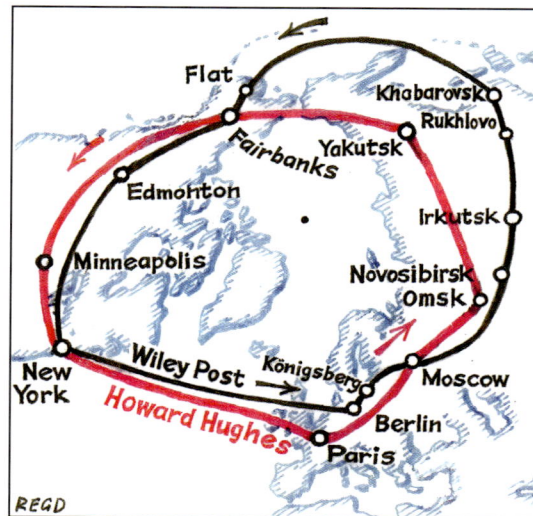

D. W. "Tommy" Tomlinson, pioneered the techniques of high altitude flying for Transcontinental & Western Air, which later became T.W.A.

Wiley Post, with his famous Lockheed Vega, Winnie Mae, which is now preserved in the Smithsonian Institution's National Air and Space Museum in Washington, D.C. Interestingly, Howard Hughes was a great admirer, and as the map shows, he was to follow closely along the same round-the-world route as Post.

Meticulous Preparation

"Our success was due to careful planning..."
— Howard Hughes

Planning, Planning, Planning...

When, after his round-the-world flight, Howard made the statement (top right), this was no exaggeration. His objective was the most carefully planned of its kind ever attempted during the Golden Age of aviation. Every conceivable emergency was considered and thoroughly discussed with the hand-picked team of experts that Howard had selected for the epic journey.

Floatation Gear

Ever fearful of a forced landing at sea, Hughes insisted on a number of modifications that would greatly improve the aircraft's flotation capability, in the event that they had to ditch the airplane. Four rubber flotation bags, which could be inflated by CO_2 cylinders, were installed in the baggage compartment; the fuel dump valves were designed so that they could be closed after the fuel was dumped (thus ingeniously converting the empty tanks into flotation chambers); and 24,000 ping-pong balls were inserted into all the empty spaces that could be found in the wing and fuselage. Two four-man inflatable life rafts were installed near the main door, along with provisions and emergency medical supplies to last for 30 days. In addition to water and canned fruit, they carried approximately seventy-five pounds of Jewish rye bread, which had been recommended by Howard's personal physician, based on its caloric content, resistance to deterioration, and palatability over a long period of time. If it became necessary to abandon the airplane in the air, five back-type parachutes were attached to the sides of the fuselage, allowing the crew to slip on the harnesses in a short time.

Navigation

The installation of the navigator's station and equipment was directed by **Harry Connor** and **Tommy Thurlow**. A special drift sight was designed and built to Thurlow's specifications and a removable hatch on top of the fuselage was provided to make celestial sightings. In addition to maps, chronometers and two bubble octants, the Lockheed 14 was equipped with a Fairchild direction finder and the newly-developed Fairchild-Maxson line of position computer. The latter eliminated the tedious mathematical tabulations that were customarily needed to calculate a position based on celestial observations.

Radio

The elaborate radio apparatus used on the flight was a combination of standard commercial equipment, together with two special units designed by **Dick Stoddart**. The mainstay of radio communication was the special 100-watt 18-frequency transmitter built by Stoddart so that the crew could remain in constant communication with flight headquarters in New York. Stoddart also designed and built an emergency radio that was placed in a water-proof flotation housing. Power for the radio was provided by a set of self-contained batteries that could be used to operate the radio for 30 hours at reduced output. It was also equipped with a hand-cranked generator that could be used in an emergency if the batteries failed or ran out of juice.

Al Lodwick's Notebook

Just before the flight, **Al Lodwick** handed Howard a small three-ringed notebook containing detailed information on each leg of the trip. In addition to information on the conditions at each airport, the personnel to be contacted, radio frequencies in use, and the availability of fuel, oil, and spare parts, Lodwick provided a set of foreign language phrases to be used in the event of a forced landing. "Where can we find an air pump to pump up our tires," was typical of the phrases that could be found in this handy translator. Nothing was left to chance. Each chapter addressed the problems that might be encountered on that particular leg of the flight. Everything from the gross weight of the airplane for take-off from Moscow, to the time allowed to be passed on the ground at the various stops: all these were included in Lodwick's little black book.

Absolutely nothing was left to chance, including this emergency radio, complete with extendable antenna. If only Amelia had carried such an item . . .

```
Page 3                    PREPARATIONS MADE

PARIS - LE BOURGET AIRPORT

ENGINE PARTS AND SERVICE (Cont.):

    Service: Wright Aeronautical Corp. have arranged
    for their service man to be available to service
    the engines on arrival. Name of man in charge of
    European Service is Vernon Ash, address Carlton
    Hotel, Amsterdam. He will either be present him-
    self or will send Mr. John (Jack) Gundlick or
    C. C. (Doc.) Maidment to Paris. Before the plane
    leaves N. Y. a cable should be sent to Mr. Ash so
    that he may have his men available.

    Oil will be drained from both engines and tanks
    upon arrival and filled with new oil.

GASOLINE AND OIL: Standard Oil Co. of N. J. have avail-
    able for our use 1750 gal. of 100 octane gasoline
    and two portable trucks, also 200 gal. D-37 oil in
    two 55 gal. drums and 18 5-gal. cans. Also 15 gal.
    Servo-Unit Oil in 2 5-gal. cans and 5 1-gal. cans.
    The name of the Standard Oil contact man is -

        Standard-Francaise de Petroles
        #1 Capt. Challe   #2 Mr. Prevost   #3 Mr. Prilliard

WATER: Standard Oil Co. have arranged to have 15 gallons
    Poland water in one or one-half gallon bottles, with
    unbroken seals.

FOOD: Standard Oil Company have made following food
    arrangements:

    12 quarts pasturized milk - in one quart sealed
        bottles
    3 lbs. fried chicken
    15 lbs. dry ice
    5 gallons of hot coffee, ready to be poured in
        ship's thermos bottles
    5 hot dinners, individually packed, consisting
        of lamb chops, baked potatoes, and fresh
        string beans, also
    Container of coffee.
```

During what is often referred to as the Golden Years of aviation — the 1920s and the 1930s — pilots too often flew "by the seat of their pants," or, at best, did little to prepare for an heroic adventure. Howard Hughes did just the opposite. He left nothing to chance, as Al Lodwick's notebook confirms. The exhibit above is only page 3.

The Team

Al Lodwick — Flight Operations Manager and Master Planner

Lodwick, an executive with the Curtiss-Wright organization, has sometimes been called Hughes's silent partner. He spent two years planning the flight and was responsible for convincing the Bureau of Air Commerce of its value to aviation so that they would issue the necessary approvals. He obtained the permissions needed to fly over all the countries along the route and took care of all the arrangements for mechanical services, supplies, customs, and visas. He was also responsible for gaining the cooperation of the New York World's Fair of 1939 — site of the flight's headquarters — and having Howard nominated as its aeronautical advisor.

W. C. "Rocky" Rockefeller — Meteorologist

The job of forecasting the weather along the flight path was entrusted to William Curtis "Rocky" Rockefeller. He was a Cal Tech graduate with a master's degree in aeronautical science and an expert meteorologist. He started working for Hughes in 1935 when he was hired as a part-time consultant for the H-1 Racer project. He was one of the leading authorities on high-altitude weather conditions, having investigated optimum flight path conditions in conjunction with Tommy Tomlinson at T.W.A. in 1934. In 1936 Rockefeller was the first recipient of the Lawrence B. Sperry Award.

Eddie Lund — Flight Engineer

The youngest of Howard's highly experienced flight crew, Lund secured his first aviation job at Clover Field in Santa Monica before he was out of his teens. He rose through several jobs before he became shop superintendent for the Timm Aircraft Corporation in 1929. He remained with the company when it was taken over by the Pacific Aermotive Corporation, which did the modification work on Hughes's S-38 amphibian in 1933. He was hired by the Hughes Aircraft Company to work on the Racer and was with them until 1937, when he was laid off and went to work for the Charles H. Babb Company at New York's Floyd Bennett Field. He took a leave of absence to accompany Howard on his round-the-world-flight.

Although Lodwick and Rockefeller did not accompany Hughes on the historic flight, they were key members of his team, and were fully recognized as such by their team leader.

Tommy Thurlow — Co-navigator

Thurlow, a recognized authority on aerial navigation, was a 33-year old Army flyer on leave from the Air Corps. A graduate of the Air Corps Technical School at Chanute Field, Illinois, he had taught celestial navigation at Rockwell Field, California, was the inventor of number of navigation aids, and headed the Instrument and Navigation Unit at the Air Corps Material Command at Wright Field, Ohio. As shown in Al Lodwick's telegram to the Army Air Corps (p. 33) his reputation had reached the Hughes organization. During the flight, Thurlow use a new type of a periscope drift meter that he had developed for determining wind drift.

Harry Connor — Co-navigator

Connor, 38, an expert navigator, had learned his trade at sea, having served as navigation officer and was a master navigator for a number of years before he began to study the problem of trans-oceanic flight. In 1929 he had acted as the navigator on the first non-stop flight from New York to Bermuda and had served as the navigator and copilot for Canadian J. Eroll Boyd's off-season flight from Montreal to London in 1930. Connor accompanied Howard on all seven of the transcontinental practice runs (five DC-1s, one S-43, and one Lockheed 14) that were conducted to develop the navigation procedures that would be used during the flight.

Dick Stoddart — Radio Engineer

Stoddart, also 38, spent eight years at sea as a radio operator until he joined the R.C.A. Company in 1927. He decided to learn how to fly after Lindbergh's famous flight and obtained his pilot's license in 1929. He then went to the National Broadcasting Company as a radio engineer in its technical department. Stoddart had previously worked with Lowell Thomas and had taken a leave of absence to participate in the Hughes flight, which would use the latest radio equipment to stay in constant communication with the project's headquarters located at the 1939 World's Fair in Flushing, New York.

Hughes's Lockheed 14-N2 Super Electra

A Very Special Airplane

The Lockheed 14 was extensively modified by a team of mechanics and engineers who worked for the Hughes Aircraft Company. Under Howard's direct (and meticulous) supervision, they built additional fuel tanks into the fuselage; placed a 79-gallon oil tank in the nose compartment; constructed radio and navigation compartments; replaced the standard nose with a Plexiglas unit that housed powerful landing lights; and installed radios, navigation gear, a Sperry gyro auto pilot; and a self-contained oxygen system. The result was referred to as the Model 14-N2.

Attention to Detail

Like the now-redundant Douglas DC-1, Howard Hughes's Lockheed was described as a **Flying Laboratory**. Compared to the radio communications equipment normally carried on a commercial airliner, or even on a rich man's private one, Howard seemed to agree with Oscar Wilde's motto: "Nothing succeeds like Excess."

Unlike Amelia Earhart who dispensed with her trailing antenna in her Lockheed 10, Howard had two, and those were in addition to the front and rear antennas shown in the drawing on this page. He also had two navigators.

There were additional gas tanks, additional oil tanks, oxygen tanks, and compartments for every accessory that might be needed on the long round-the-world flight.

An Impressive Airplane

The standard Super Electra was a little larger than Earhart's Electra (see tabulation on page 39) and its certified take-off weight was, at 20,000 lb. (ten tons), more than twice that of its predecessor. Hughes added another 5,000 lb. to the 14-N's all-up weight (mostly fuel), but added another 200 hp to the Wright Cyclone engines to take care of the take-off performance and the weight of the extra fuel. The emphasis on fuel was paramount in the calculations.

Howard had already come near to losing his life once through running out of fuel. He was not going to do so again, and, for the rest of his flying career, he was obsessively meticulous about details of operation.

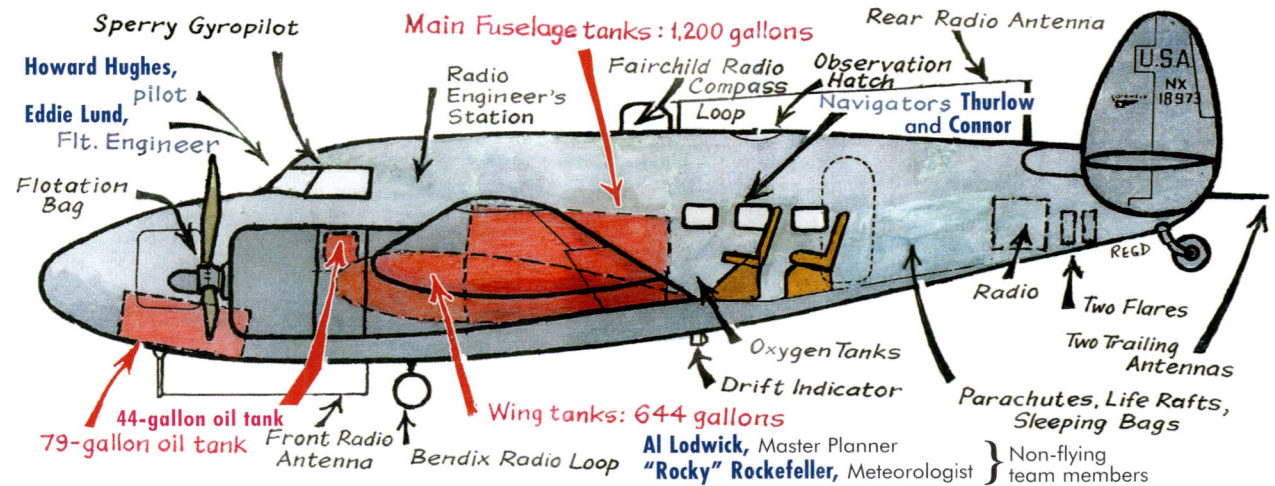

Sperry Gyropilot
Howard Hughes, pilot
Eddie Lund, Flt. Engineer
Flotation Bag
Radio Engineer's Station
Main Fuselage tanks: 1,200 gallons
Fairchild Radio Compass Loop
Observation Hatch
Rear Radio Antenna
U.S.A NX 18973
Navigators Thurlow and Connor
REG'D
Radio
Two Flares
Two Trailing Antennas
44-gallon oil tank
79-gallon oil tank
Front Radio Antenna
Bendix Radio Loop
Wing tanks: 644 gallons
Oxygen Tanks
Drift Indicator
Parachutes, Life Rafts, Sleeping Bags
Al Lodwick, Master Planner
"Rocky" Rockefeller, Meteorologist
} Non-flying team members

Howard had every reason to be satisfied with the extent of the preparations made.

The flight deck of the Hughes Lockheed 14. (Florida Air Museum)

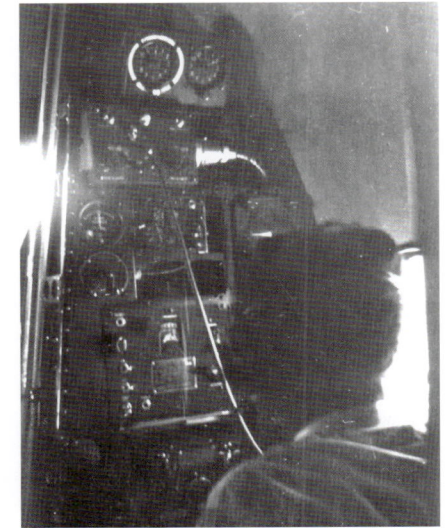

The radio operator's station on the Hughes Lockheed 14. (Florida Air Museum)

Across the Atlantic

Invitation to a Fair

Howard Hughes and his four-man flight crew took off from Burbank on the Fourth of July 1938 and headed across country to Floyd Bennett Field in Brooklyn — the starting point for the first leg of their round-the world flight. As his crew made final preparations for the flight, Howard spent the next few days dodging newspapermen and photographers. The flight was scheduled to depart on Saturday, 9 July, but when the big day arrived, Howard was chagrined to discover that a number of the engine cylinders had become pitted. He and his crew had no choice but to stand by while a gang of mechanics worked feverishly to replace the defective cylinders. Howard hoped to take off at dawn the next day, but he left the airfield when it became apparent that the repairs would not be completed in time.

By the time he returned to the Floyd Bennett, late on Sunday afternoon, a large crowd of reporters, photographers, and newsreel men were milling about the hangar where the Lockheed 14 was parked. **Grover Whalen**, president of the World's Fair Corporation, was standing at a microphone, waiting to greet Howard and his crew. Already a prominent politician, businessman, and public relations specialist, Whalen won fame as New York City's chief of police when he declared that, "There is plenty of law at the end of a nightstick." He was later appointed by Fiorello LaGuardia as New York's official greeter and became a public celebrity, easily recognized by his exquisitely-groomed moustache and ever-present carnation boutonniere

As Howard approached the microphone, Whalen handed him a bundle of letters to be delivered to the heads of European governments, inviting foreign airmen to visit the World's Fair. He praised the crew, and christened the Lockheed the *New York World's Fair 1939*. Wearing his now famous "lucky" brown fedora, Howard was impatient to get under way as he waited for the end of the speech. When Whalen was finished he asked Howard to say a few words. Hughes nervously pulled a piece of paper from his pocket and addressed the crowd, expressing the hope that the flight would further international cooperation and friendship.

Just as the ceremonies were breaking up, a young woman skipped through the crowd and pressed a wad of chewing gum to the airplane's tail. She was Mrs. Harry Connor. "That's for good luck," she told the reporters. "I told Harry to be sure and bring it back to me."

Take-off

After the ceremony ended, Howard Hughes and his crew prepared to get under way. Howard started the engines and taxied to the north end of the airstrip. At 7:19 p.m., he opened the throttles and went roaring down the 3,500-foot concrete runway (it was the only hard-surfaced runway in New York). The Lockheed's tail hit the end of the runway and bumped on to an area of dirt and grass, throwing up clouds of dust, before it slowly eased into the air.

Hughes turned to the northeast into the gathering dusk. Like Lindbergh, Howard had chosen to follow the great circle route to Paris. The flight path would take him and his crew over Boston, Cape Breton Island, and Newfoundland. From there it was 1,800 miles to Ireland.

Another Record

As they winged their way over the Atlantic, Stoddart exchanged greetings with ocean liners and maintained continual contact with flight headquarters in New York. At 10:30 p.m., he even arranged a radio hook-up with the Columbia Broadcasting System.

Hughes landed at Le Bourget Airport at 4:58 p.m. on Monday, 11 July 1938. He had made the crossing in sixteen hours, thirty-eight minutes cutting Lindbergh's record in half. A light drizzle was falling as Hughes brought the airplane to a gentle stop in front of the airport's main building, where the U.S. ambassador and a throng of dignitaries were waiting to greet the team. Thousands of Parisians showed up to get a glimpse of the airplane and its courageous crew. Howard had planned to take off again within two hours, but bad weather over Germany, combined with the discovery of a crack in the fuselage — probably caused when the airplane bumped the runway on take-off — caused him to delay the flight until repairs were made and the weather improved.

The Lockheed bearing the name New York World's Fair 1939. (Lakeland Library)

The Lockheed taking off from Floyd Bennett Field. (Lakeland Library)

In the beaten-up "lucky" fedora, Howard inspected the Lockheed soon after landing in Paris. (Lakeland Public Library)

Across the Soviet Union

Americans were following the flight step by step. It made the headlines every day and was the lead story on radio newscasts. Howard Hughes—movie producer, pilot, airplane designer—already a romantic personality — was becoming an even greater national hero.

On to Moscow

The rain did not stop until well after midnight, but a strong cross-wind nearly caused a disaster. The aircraft's left wheel hit a rut at the far end of the field, and they took several hard bounces before Hughes managed to get the heavily-loaded airplane into the air. Fears that the landing gear had been damaged during the takeoff thankfully proved unfounded when Howard made a perfect landing at Moscow Airport at 11:13 a.m. on Tuesday, 12 July. The Russians were waiting with a 2,500-gallon tank-car, full of high-octane aviation gasoline, a box of American corn flakes for breakfast, and a large jar of caviar as a going-away gift, which Howard politely declined, exclaiming that "every pound counts." After two hours on the ground, they winged their way to Omsk, 1,300 miles from Moscow, and another 8 hours of flying.

Across Siberia — with Diversion

Hughes landed the *New York World's Fair 1939* on the grass landing strip at Omsk at dawn. The flight plan had originally called for a landing at Novosibirsk, but heavy rains had flooded the airstrip, forcing a change in landing sites. Fueling at Omsk took more than four hours to complete because of the poor quality of the gasoline. It had to be carefully strained to remove foreign matter and treated with ethyl (tetraethyl lead) to increase the octane rating. They carried supplies of the octane-boosting additive along with a fine wire mesh funnel just for such an eventuality. Howard supervised every minute of the refueling.

He was not one to always follow generally accepted flight procedures. He had a habit of shutting down the engines—to let the cylinder heads cool down—after he had taxied into takeoff position. This almost resulted in tragedy. While he was waiting for the heads to cool, a vicious thunderstorm struck. Impatient to get away, he decided to take off in the heavy downpour. The field was already soft from previous rains, and he reached the end of the field at minimum flying speed in a near-stalled condition. One wing almost dug in, recalled Dick Stoddart. Howard managed to climb out, but — unusually for him — was so shaken by the event that he remained fixated, staring straight ahead for the next ten minutes. The rest of the ten and a half-hour flight to Yakutsk, in northeast Siberia, was uneventful. They stopped just long enough to refuel before taking off for Fairbanks, Alaska.

Return to New York

The aviators touched down at Fairbanks 3 days and 57 minutes after leaving New York. Among the greeters awaiting them was **Mrs. Wiley Post**, widow of the flier whose record they were breaking. Howard warmly received her, expressing his sincere admiration for her late husband's previous feat.

The weather to New York was uncertain when they took off again at 8:36 p.m. Because of a storm they by-passed Winnipeg, stopping instead at Minneapolis the next morning. They refueled in just 33 minutes — the shortest pit stop of the entire flight — and were soon headed towards New York and a new record for a round-the-world flight.

French soldiers guarding the New York World's Fair 1939 *during its stop over in Paris. (Lakeland Library)*

Howard supervises the mechanics as they service the New York World's Fair 1939 *during the brief refueling stop in Moscow. (Lakeland Public Library)*

Somewhere He Must Be Sayin'—
By Reg Manning — Arizona Republic Staff Artist

WELL, WILEY – WE DON'T NEED T'WORRY ABOUT TH' FUTURE OF AVIATION— LOOKS LIKE WE LEFT IT IN PRETTY GOOD HANDS!

NYC Mayor LaGuardia greets the unshaven Howard Hughes as he emerges from the Lockheed 14 upon returning to Floyd Bennett Field on 14 July 1938. L-R: Dick Stoddart, Howard Hughes, the Mayor, Harry Connor, Grover Whalen. (Lakeland Library)

Round-the-World Triumph

Back to the Starting Point

Twenty thousand people were on hand to greet the *New York World's Fair 1939* when it touched down at Floyd Bennett Field at 3:37 p.m. on Thursday afternoon, 14 July 1938. Hughes and his team had set a new record, circling the globe in 3 days, 19 hours, and 17 minutes, according to the official flight log prepared by Lodwick. (The total elapsed time was 91 hours, 14 minutes, 10 seconds — see opposite page).

The crowd rushed towards the airplane as soon as Howard taxied it to a stop and shut down the engines. Mayor Fiorello LaGuardia, and the president of New York's World Fair, Grover Whalen, along with dozens of reporters and hundreds of spectators, were waiting to greet him when he emerged from the aircraft. With the police half dragging them through the rambunctious throng, Howard and his four-man crew were taken to a nearby press tent where a brief radio interview was conducted before the crowd became too unruly. Whalen quickly hustled Hughes and the official party into waiting limousines that whisked them into Manhattan.

A Hero's Welcome

The next day, Howard was treated to the traditional hero's welcome of a ticker-tape parade. More than a million people lined Broadway as he and his crewmen passed by in open cars. Howard waved constantly and was smiling broadly by the time the procession reached City Hall, where he and his crew were presented with the Key to the City.

After some introductory remarks by the assembled dignitaries, Howard moved towards the microphone. Nervously, he fumbled with some handwritten notes that he pulled from his pocket, before he slowly began to address the crowd in a clear, steady voice. I am not good at making speeches, he told them, but

> "I want everyone to know that the flight was not a stunt, but was carried out according to a carefully prepared plan. We who did it are entitled to no particular credit. We are no supermen or anything of that sort. If credit is due to anyone, it should go to the men who designed the modern American flying machine and its equipment."

Tributes to the Crew and Wiley Post

Howard once again praised those who had contributed to the flight. Please remember, he said,

> "that I am but one of five persons who made that trip, and being taller than any of them I kept getting in the way and making a nuisance of myself. If you must praise anyone, save your shouts for Wiley Post, for by flying around the world, in the time he did and with but one eye, he made the most amazing flight that has ever occurred."

After more festivities in Washington and Chicago. On 30 July, Howard flew the Lockheed into Houston for the most tumultuous reception of all. A quarter of a million people turned out to shower Hughes and his crew with confetti and cheers.

That evening, Howard disappeared. A frantic effort was made to locate him, until Sherman Fairchild discovered Howard in the men's room, locked in one of the stalls, writing his after-dinner speech on toilet paper.

Accolades

Howard Hughes had become an American hero. At 32 years of age he had achieved one of his three great ambitions: he was the most famous aviator in the world. Al Lodwick had worked diligently behind the scenes to ensure that Hughes received the honors he deserved. These included a **second Harmon Trophy**, the **Octave Chanute Award**, and the even more prestigious **Collier Trophy**, awarded for significant achievement in the advancement of aviation. Lodwick also helped to persuade the U.S. Congress to award Hughes a special gold medal in recognition of his contributions to the science of aviation.

The Limelight Fades

Howard had landed in New York on 14 July 1938. Only a year later, on 3 September 1939, Britain and France declared war, so that much of the recognition of Hughes's achievement did not receive the world-wide attention that it deserved. In 1938 there was no television, newsreels were selective, and ships still took a week to cross the Atlantic.

Ringed about by reporters, policemen and the privileged few, Howard Hughes' Lockheed 14 Super Electra, (New York World's Fair 1939) rests on the runway before the administration building at Floyd Bennett Field after circling the globe in 3 days, 19 hours and 17 minutes. While the officials greet Hughes and his four companions, 20,000 spectators mass behind the barrier at either side. (Library of Congress)

Howard Hughes's ticker-tape parade down Broadway was greater than Charles Lindbergh's — if the collection of the ticker-tape afterwards is a measure of the accolade.

The Great Flight of 1938

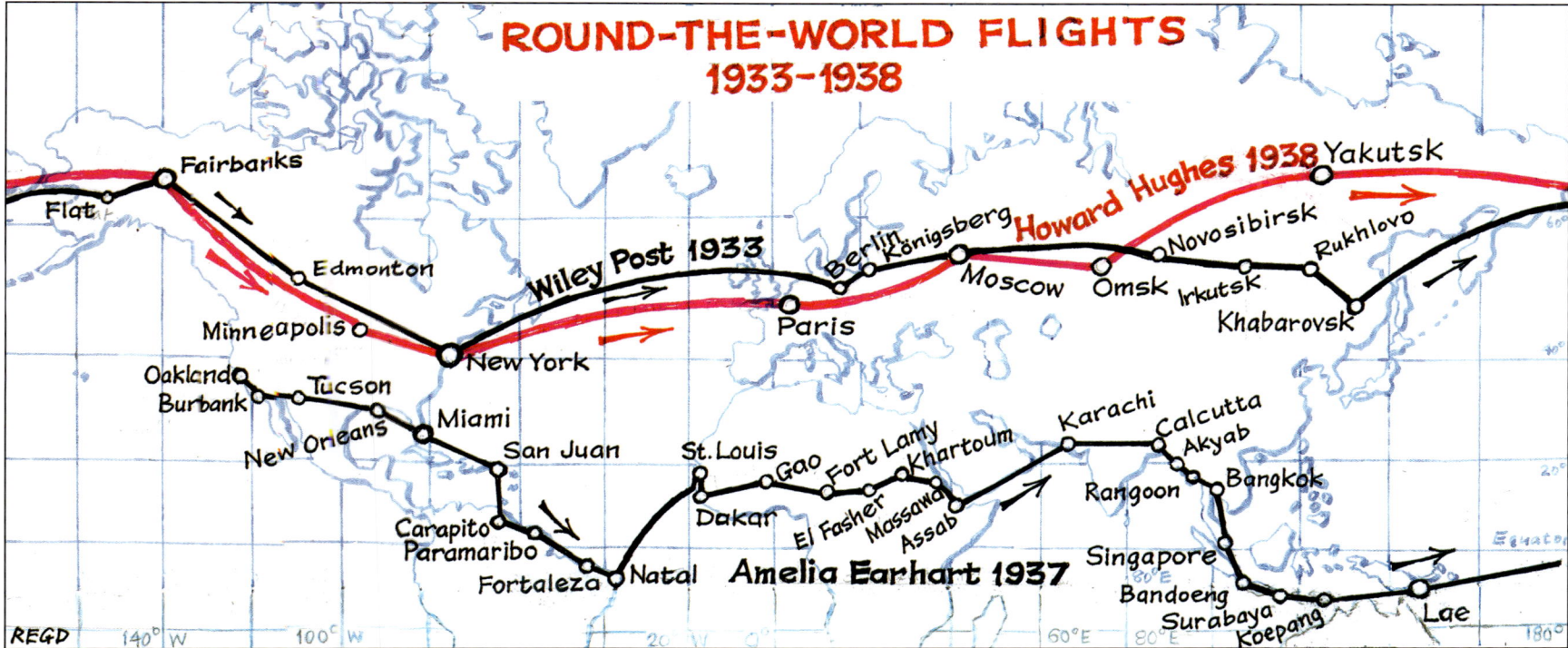

ROUND-THE-WORLD FLIGHTS 1933–1938

Flat · Fairbanks · Edmonton · Minneapolis · Oakland · Burbank · Tucson · New Orleans · Miami · San Juan · Carapito · Paramaribo · Fortaleza · Natal · New York · St.Louis · Gao · Fort Lamy · Khartoum · Dakar · El Fasher · Massawa · Assab · Paris · Berlin · Königsberg · Moscow · Omsk · Irkutsk · Novosibirsk · Rukhlovo · Khabarovsk · Yakutsk · Karachi · Calcutta · Akyab · Rangoon · Bangkok · Singapore · Bandoeng · Surabaya · Koepang · Lae

Wiley Post 1933 — Howard Hughes 1938 — Amelia Earhart 1937

REGD

LOG OF HOWARD HUGHES'S ROUND THE WORLD FLIGHT

Date	Place	Time of Take-Off E.S.T.	Time of Arrival E.S.T.	Distance (Great Cicle) (miles)	Time in Air	Time on Ground	Average Speed in Flight (mph)
July 10	New York	8:20 p.m.	—	—	—	—	—
July 11	Paris	7:24 p.m.	10:55 a.m.	3,641	16 hr. 35 m.	8 hr. 29 m.	219.6
July 12	Moscow	5:30 a.m.	3:13 a.m.	1,557	7 hr. 49 m.	2 hr. 17 m.	200
July 12	Omsk	5:37 p.m.	1:00 p.m.	1,400	7 hr. 30 m.	4 hr. 37 m.	186.7
July 13	Yakutsk	7:01 a.m.	4:03 a.m.	2,158	10 hr. 31 m.	2 hr. 53 m.	205.1
July 13	Fairbanks	8:36 p.m.	7:18 p.m.	2,456	12 hr. 17 m.	1 hr. 18 m.	200
July 14	Minneapolis	9:11 a.m.	8:38 a.m.	2,483	12 hr. 2 m.	33 m.	207
July 14	New York	—	1:34 p.m.	1,017	4 hr. 23 m.	—	232

Total distance (Great Circle Route) 14,712 miles
Total elapsed time 91 hrs, 14 mins, 10 secs [less than 4 days]

Average speed, inc. stops 161.3 mph
Total time in flight 71 hrs, 7 mins
Average speed in flight 206.9 mph

Howard Buys An Airline

Howard Meets an Old Friend

Late in December 1938, or early January 1939, **Jack Frye**, the president of **Transcontinental & Western Air (T.W.A.)**, and his associate, **Paul Richter**, flew to Los Angeles for a meeting with Howard Hughes. John Hertz, the fiscally conservative chairman of the board of directors had refused to approve payment for the four-engined Boeing 307s that Frye was trying to acquire for the airline. Jack Frye was a childhood friend of Howard's and he was well aware of the millionaire's insatiable interest in aviation. The two men were not close friends, but they both loved flying. This made it easy for Frye to approach Hughes with his problems.

A New Obsession

What exactly transpired during their day-long meeting is not known. Some say that Frye asked Howard to buy the airline; others say it was Howard's idea. In any case, Howard was captivated by the idea of owning an airline. He immediately agreed to purchase 100,000 shares of T.W.A. stock and had acquired enough shares by the end of January 1939 to challenge Hertz for control of the airline. Hertz caved in, selling his shares to Hughes, thus giving him control of the airline. Howard continued to buy shares on the open market until he owned 78 percent of the company's stock.

Howard may not have been a championship golfer (although his handicap was 1), but he had already achieved one of his youthful ambitions. He had become the best pilot in the world. Now, he was offered one of the biggest airlines in the world, and as always he never did anything by halves — he set out to make T.W.A. the biggest airline in the world.

Transcontinental & Western Air

Howard Hughes was not starting from scratch. By 1939, the U.S. airline industry had progressed enormously since its formative years in the late 1920s and early 1930s. Interestingly, the new owner had brushed shoulders with T.W.A. when he flew the Northrop Gamma and the epochal Douglas DC-1. This latter airliner, (Charles Lindbergh was T.W.A.'s technical adviser) had elevated T.W.A. into the front line of United States airlines. It had been formed in 1930 by the "Shotgun Marriage" of Transcontinental Air Transport (T.A.T.) and Western Air Express (W.A.E.) to form one of the three transcontinental airlines, planned by Postmaster General Walter F. Brown, who was the architect of the U.S. airline system.

Howard had all the ingredients that are necessary for an airline to succeed: substantial capital, efficient airplanes, and a good route network. To quote a British commentator, he inherited a great airline, and then set out to make it greater.

Jack Frye was a childhood friend of Howard Hughes. A licensed transport pilot, he had been running T.W.A. since 1934 and was instrumental in creating the specifications for the DC-1, the first of the extraordinarily successful series of twin-engine Douglas transports.

As mentioned above, Howard Hughes took over an airline with a good network. In the course of fashioning a transcontinental route, T.W.A. had included almost every major population center of the United States, with the exception of Detroit, Boston, and Washington/Baltimore.

Boeing Stratoliner

Flying "Above the Weather"

The Boeing 307 Stratoliner was the world's first pressurized airliner. It was an offshoot of the B-17, using many of its components — landing gear, wing, tail and engines — attached to a radically different fuselage. T.W.A. had ordered six Stratoliners on 29 January 1937, but Boeing had cancelled the order after T.W.A. defaulted on the progress payments — because of Hertz's intransigence — that were required under the original contract.

Howard Checks Out on the 307

After taking financial control of T.W.A., Howard Hughes and Glenn Odekirk flew up to Seattle to inspect the prototype and to re-negotiate the terms of T.W.A.'s original contract. Hughes arranged to finance all six through the Hughes Tool Company and bought one of the six 307s for his personal use. He returned in July, to be checked out in the 307 — the first four-engined aircraft that he had piloted. George W. Haldeman, the Civil Aeronautics Authority pilot in charge of the flight, was impressed with Howard's piloting skills and his ability to grasp the flying characteristics of the 307 so quickly.

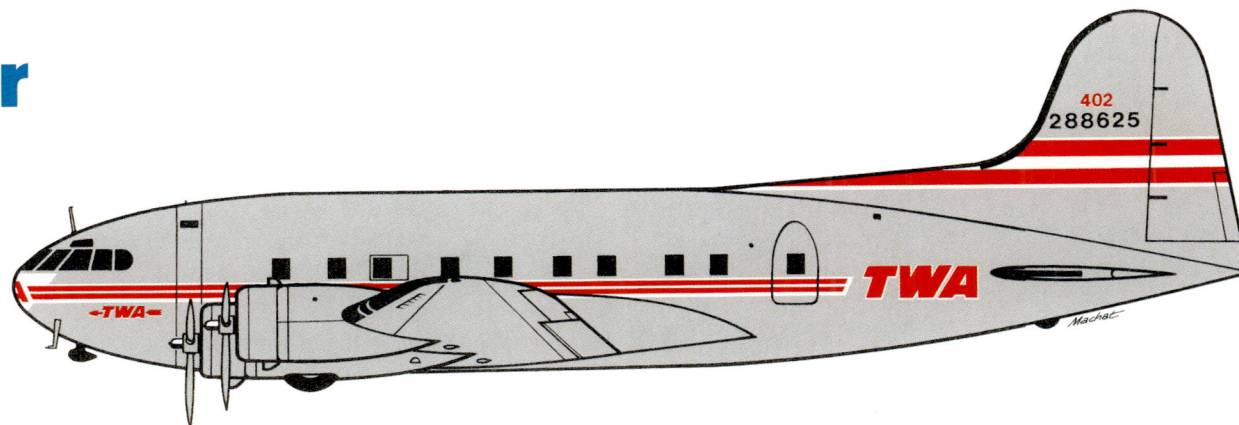

Howard must have been delighted, not only to take over a prestigous airline, but to initiate a technical step forward in airliner technology, viz. the pressurization of the cabin that would allow flying at a higher altitude, thus permitting smoother flight "above the weather."

Length	74 ft
Wing Span	107 ft
Engine	Wright R-1820 (900 hp) x 2
Seating	33
Cruise Speed	220 mph
MGTOW	42,000 lb.
Range	2,390 miles

Size comparison with Constellation (p.55)

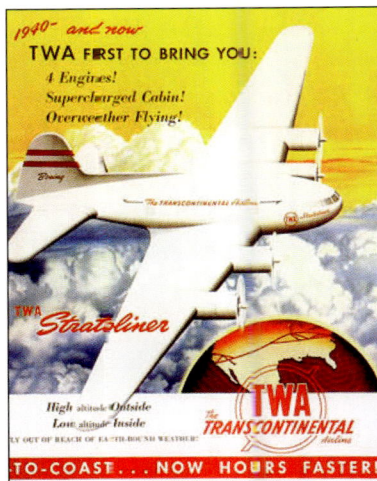

Because of the outbreak of the Second World War, the Boeing Stratoliner, which went into service in 1940, was not in T.W.A. domestic service for very long. But the airline made the most of its flagship status.

Above: After modifications for certification (note the addition of the dorsal fin), the Boeing 307 heralded a new generation of commercial airliners.

Left: Howard Hughes photographed during his 5 July 1939 visit to the Boeing plant in Seattle to inspect the Stratoliner. (Author's Collection)

A New Airliner Generation

Single-Engined to Twin and Tri-motor

During the years of progress in the annals of air transport, after the end of the Great War of 1914–18, the world's aviation industry converted "guns into ploughshares," and certain aircraft were more than improved variants of existing types. In 1919, in Europe, the all-metal **Junkers-F 13** was technically far in advance of all its steel-framed wood-and-fabric contemporaries. Similarly, in the late 1920s, the **Ford Tri-Motor** in the United States and the **Fokker F.VII** series in Europe combined size and comfort to claim superiority. In 1952, the **Junkers-Ju 52/3m** gained temporary ascendancy in Europe until it was outclassed by the American twin-engined series which began with the **Douglas DC-1** in 1933.

The developed version of the DC-1, the famous **DC-3**, was so superior to all rivals that, for the first time, European airline leaders crossed the Atlantic to knock on Douglas's door. They were stimulated by the sensational performance of the Dutch airline **K.L.M.** in the England-Australia Air Race when its DC-2, complete with passengers and mail, was a close second to the specially-designed racing airplane that won the race.

The success of the Douglas design was thus demonstrated beyond all doubt by a widely-publicized event. The manufacturer could not have had better publicity agents than K.L.M. and its visionary leader, **Dr. Plesman**, who even had to overcome understandable national pride by replacing the best that the Dutch Fokker company could offer.

Four-engined Long Range

There were parallels to this combination of factors when the next generation of commercial airliners superseded the Douglas twin-engined types in size and range. The German **Focke-Wulf Fw 200 Condor** landplane, which made the round-trip non-stop crossing from Berlin to New York in 1938, heralded the demise of the big flying boats. The **Boeing 307 Stratoliner**, which went into service in 1940, was bigger, and it was the world's first pressurized airliner; but it did not have the transcontinental range to fly with payload without two or more stops. During the war, its pressurization equipment was removed to allow for the weight of the extra fuel needed to cross the Atlantic Ocean. Then an element of luck was combined with the same kind of vision that had made K.L.M. the finest airline in Europe.

A Little Luck and Howard Hughes

Luck has been defined as "when opportunity comes face to face with preparation." In this case, the luck was with Lockheed, because Boeing, Douglas, and Consolidated were heavily burdened with military production of bombers for the Second World War. Its Burbank factory was prepared, because designers Hall Hibbard and Kelly Johnson had, in 1939, already offered the 34-seat, 300 mph, **Model 44 Excalibur** to the industry.

To this combination of opportunity and preparation was then added a third, essential, ingredient, the vision of **Howard Hughes**. He it was who realized that both the Boeing 307 and the Excalibur were not big enough for T.W.A., the airline he owned, nor could they cross the Atlantic with full payload, even with intermediate stops in Newfoundland and/or Ireland.

Behold the Constellation

And just as Dr. Plesman and K.L.M. had proved a point in 1934, Howard Hughes did the same ten years later with the Lockheed Constellation. With determination, conviction (and the money to back up his instincts) he insisted on a challenging specification for a superior airplane that, as with Douglas in 1934 was so good that the airline world beat a pathway to Lockheed's door, and British historian Peter Brooks would ruefully describe the "Connie" as "America's Secret Weapon" (see page 54).

The Lockheed Model 049 Constellation crowned a new generation of four-engined long-haul airliners that, in contrast to the DC-3 generation that preceded it, could cross oceans, carry twice as many people, fly almost twice as fast, and (as the cabin was pressurized) offer far greater comfort.

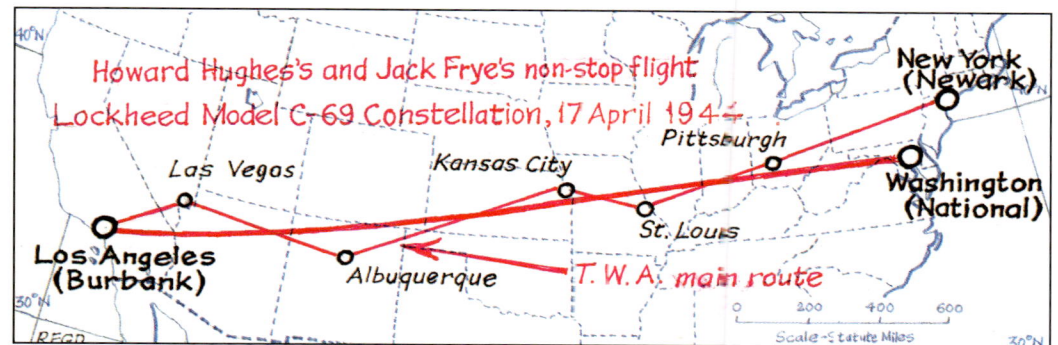

Howard Hughes's and Jack Frye's non-stop flight Lockheed Model C-69 Constellation, 17 April 1944

T.W.A. main route

Howard Hughes launched the Constellation with great flair. In delivering it to the authorities in Washington, he had — contrary to wide-spread assumptions — permission to paint the C-69 military version in T.W.A.'s colors, and to be able to deliver the aircraft personally.

Red Letter Day

Dramatic Debut

After its first flight, on 9 January 1943, the Constellation's performance (see page 55) was so satisfactory that it made five more flights on the same day. Such a debut would not have been possible without the persistence of Howard Hughes, who had been able to combine his great wealth and airline ownership with his technical knowledge and, above all, a vision of the future growth and extent of world airline passenger traffic.

Howard proved his point dramatically with his non-stop flight from Burbank to Washington in 1944. In addition to the five-man crew, the military C-69 Constellation carried twelve passengers, including seven from T.W.A. (and Ava Gardner was rumored to be on board as a supernumerary crew member). The flight was as far-reaching in importance in the record of aeronautical achievement as Charles Lindbergh's New York-Paris non-stop flight of 1927. Without Howard Hughes, there would never have been a Lockheed Constellation, and without the Constellation, the post-war generation of trans-ocean pressurized airliners would have taken a less ambitious course towards the future..

The Greatest Moment

If ever there was a "red letter day" (a reference to special days marked in red in calendars) in Howard Hughes's eventful life, it must have been 17 April 1944; and even though he was greeted by General Arnold (see page 54) the greatest moment must have been when, before the microphones, he presented the Lockheed Constellation to the United States Government in person.

The photograph on this page captures the moment, when Howard, looking even younger than his 39 years, and his partner and co-pilot, Jack Frye, is talking to Jesse Jones, President Roosevelt's Secretary of Commerce, with a rather austere William Burden, the Assistant Secretary at his side.

There had been other Great Moments for Hughes, for example when he made speed records, and especially when he flew around the world in four days in 1938, to be celebrated with a ticker-tape parade in New York. But this was different. This event was not for personal glory or for another trophy. It was for the benefit of the air travelling public, as

he himself declared in a press interview, quoted verbatim on page 55.

The Moment in Perspective

Other great events in the chronology of aviation history were "red letter days." The Montgolfier brothers' balloon flight of 1783 was perhaps the first, and in modern times the flight of the Wright brothers in 1903 paved the way for controlled airplane operations. Bleriot's crossing of the English Channel is well remembered, although Igor Sikorsky's St. Petersburg-Kiev flight of 1914 — by the world's first transport airplane — is not. The British mark Alcock and Brown's first non-stop 1919 Atlantic crossing, while Charles Lindbergh's New York-Paris nonstop flight of 1927 was truly remarkable, as was the Australian Kingsford Smith's trans-Pacific flight of 1928.

Other long-distance performances during the early 1930s attracted much public attention, but 1934 was a "red-letter year" — it this derivative term can be coined. The England-Australia Air Race demonstrated that commercial aircraft could match even the best racing designs in speed and range; Pan American Airways inaugurated the world's first trans-ocean commercial air route, and T.W.A. introduced the Douglas DC-2 for its passenger service.

A Many-Faceted Triumph

The landing in Washington early in the afternoon of 17 April 1944 echoed in many ways that of K.L.M.'s DC-2 in 1934; as the achievement was not for personal gain but for the benefit of commercial aviation as a whole. Both the DC-2 and the Constellation carried passengers, not just the pilots and crew. The latter was also pressurized, and like the twin-engined Douglas before it, started a new era in aircraft manufacturing technology.

Furthermore, the Constellation was not only a big airplane, it was, by the standards of the day, a "hot ship." In 1935, in a Vultee, Andrews and Snead has crossed the continent in 10 hours, 22 minutes, averaging 222 mph. Howard Hughes flew his H-1B from Burbank to Newark in 1937 in 7 hours 28 minutes at 327 mph (see page 31). Howard and Frye beat the U.S. transcontinental record in 6 hours 58 minutes at 355 mph.

Only two years later, with the Second World War ended, the Constellation was in commercial service. Unlike Nazi Germany's wartime V1 and V2 secret weapons, this was indeed the peacetime secret weapon of the United States. It led the way in American world supremacy in commercial airliner manufacture for the next half-century.

This was the historic moment that set the seal on Howard Hughes's outstanding achievement in delivering the Lockheed Constellation to the authorities in Washington. The authorities are represented (left to right) by William Burden, Assistant Secretary of Commerce, and Jesse Jones, his chief, who had formerly been in charge of the Reconstruction Finance Corporation (R.F.C.), an integral part of President Roosevelt's New Deal. The relatively young Howard Hughes and his casually-dressed co-pilot Jack Frye are there to clinch this particular deal.

Secret Weapon

Blueprint for an Airliner

Before the first of T.W.A.'s Stratoliners was delivered, Howard Hughes began to think about developing a new high-speed, super-deluxe, pressurized, four-engined airliner with transcontinental range that would give T.W.A. an advantage over the competition. In April 1939, Howard called Jack Frye to discuss the project reportedly for more than eight hours. By the end of their conversation, Howard Hughes and Jack Frye had agreed on the design characteristics for a radically new airliner (later to be named the Constellation and which her crews would lovingly nickname the "Connie"). It would fly at 20,000 feet altitude — "above the weather" like the 307 — but was larger and better, and able to carry 50 passengers and 6,000 pounds of cargo nonstop across the continental U.S.A. It would be T.W.A.'s secret weapon against all the other competing airlines.

Lockheed Meets the Challenge

The onset of the Second World War in Europe in 1939 foresaw possible American future military involvement, Boeing was producing the B-17 bomber, so Howard approached Consolidated Aircraft, but Reuben Fleet, the firm's president, said it would be too risky. With memories of the L-14's engineering, Howard approached Jack Gross, president of Lockheed Aircraft, who agreed to a meeting at his Muirfield Road home in the Hancock Park section of Los Angeles. Hall Hibbard, Lockheed's chief engineer, and Kelly Johnson, the company's lead designer, were the only others present.

Historic Purchase

After several weeks of negotiations and technical discussions, Hughes, Frye, and Gross reached an agreement on the final details of the contract. Only Howard had both the financial muscle and the inclination to sign the $18 million deal, which was then the largest contract in commercial aviation history. He agreed to buy the first forty airplanes from Lockheed, provided that the development was conducted in the utmost secrecy with the planes going exclusively to T.W.A., thus giving the airline a two-year lead over the competition. Hughes Tool Company would purchase the $425,000 airplanes, which it would then lease to T.W.A.

Whether deliberate or not, this was a neat reversal of Boeing's action in 1933 when it refused to share the initial order for Boeing 247s with Jack Frye at T.W.A. Without Hughes, there would not have been a Constellation, and Boeing's post-war re-entry into the commercial market and its market share would have been far different.

Commercial Airliner to Military Transport

The development of the Lockheed Model 49, as the Constellation was officially known, was therefore conducted in great secrecy until Lockheed was forced to divulge its work to the War Production Board in May 1941. The announcement and photographs of the Constellation, electrified the industry. Its long-range, high-speed, and high-altitude capabilities far exceeded those of any existing commercial transport.

When the production of commercial airliners was suspended at the outbreak of the Second World War, the Constellation program was turned over to the Army Air Forces for series production of the C-69 transport. During the negotiations with the Army, Howard astutely worked out an ingenious agreement that gave T.W.A. jurisdiction over the first prototype off the production line so that the airline could conduct acceptance and shakedown flights of the Constellation before turning it over to the Army. The deal gave Howard the opportunity to orchestrate another great publicity event while, at the same time setting yet another transcontinental flight record.

Moment of Triumph

On 17 April 1944, Howard Hughes and Jack Frye took off for Washington, D.C., where the new airliner would receive its public debut. Howard would have the honor of landing the airplane in Washington when they touched down. They set a new transcontinental speed record for a commercial transport of 6 hours 58 minutes. To the chagrin of the Army brass, the airplane was dressed in the airline's distinctive color scheme, bearing the T.W.A. logo on its nose, and the airline's slogan "The Transcontinental Airline" prominently displayed in the center of the fuselage.

The New York Times hailed the flight as an "outline of the shape of things to come," but "Hap" Arnold, the Chief of the Army Air Force, was furious at the publicity garnered for the airline. His demeanor did not improve when Howard spent several more days demonstrating the Constellation to high government officials — including the entire Civil Aeronautics Board — instead of transferring the C-69 immediately to the Air Force, as stipulated in the contract.

Howard Hughes and Jack Frye arrive in Washington after flying the Constellation from Burbank to claim a transcontinental record. (T.W.A. archives)

Howard Hughes is seen here just after taking General "Hap" Arnold on a demonstration flight over Washington, DC. (R.E.G. Davies collection)

Lockheed Model 049 Constellation

An Idea Born of near-Tragedy

During his record-setting transcontinental flight in the H-1, Hughes had had a lot of trouble at high altitude with his oxygen system. He had flown for several hours and he was on the verge of unconsciousness, in danger of freezing to death. The experience gave him an idea. He dreamed of an airplane that would permit passengers to fly at the same high speed and at the same altitude, but with a difference: the flight would be in perfect comfort. He kept thinking about what could be done if an airline put enough effort into such an ambitious project.

When Jack Frye, T.W.A.'s embattled president, came to him complaining about conservative stockholders of T.W.A. and their unsympathetic view of the future of air transport, he immediately caught the millionaire flyer's interest. As Hughes later told a reporter during one of his rare interviews:

I thought of TWA as the implement for vast development and improvement in passenger airplanes and transport. It wasn't so much the details of airline operation that interested me — such as food, ticketing and passenger handling. It was instead, the possibility of tremendous advances in the technical side of air transportation — for greater speeds, altitude, range, safety, and passenger comfort.

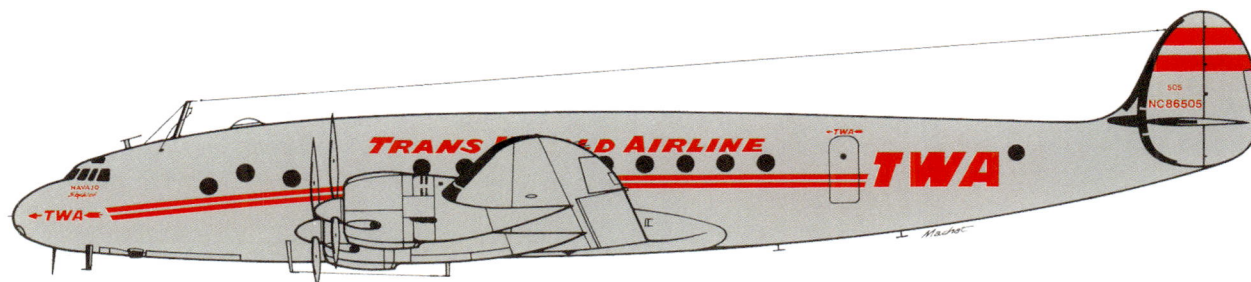

Other long-range four-engined airliners entered service after the end of the Second World War, but none excelled the Constellation in public acclaim.

Length	95 ft
Wing Span	123 ft
Engine	Wright R-3350 (2,200 hp) x 4
Seating	54
Cruise Speed	300 mph
MGTOW	86,250 lb.
Range	2,290 miles

Basis for size comparison with other landplanes in this book.

Historic Debut: The Secret Weapon Leaves the Hangar

Picture of Elegance: The Constellation over New York

New Directions

A Friend in Need

Howard Hughes knew many people and had many contacts in the aviation industry. One of the closest was **Sherman Fairchild**, an inventor and entrepreneur who owned several companies in the aviation business, and who was a frequent social companion of Howard's. Like Hughes, Fairchild was an aviation pioneer who sought commercial success. The two men had much in common and shared similar interests. They were deeply involved in aviation, were enthralled with technology, and both had an insatiable appetite for pursuing new ideas. Both men were wealthy, unattached, good looking, and single, and both were captivated by beautiful women.

Duramold

In the summer of 1939, and, though wealthy, Sherman was short of the substantial amount of cash needed to expand his aircraft company, and offered Howard the opportunity to purchase an exclusive license for the **Duramold** process. One of the Fairchild subsidiary companies had been developing this as an alternative to the highly expensive, labor intensive, all-metal, riveted construction that had become the standard method in the aircraft manufacturing business.

The Duramold process consisted of resin-impregnated layers of wood veneer that were molded together under pressure. Duramold appeared to be an attractive material that would reduce the cost of aircraft manufacturing by eliminating the time consuming and labor-intensive riveting that was needed to join aluminum parts together. It also produced a much smother aerodynamic surface than could be achieved using riveted aluminum. This latter quality must have been especially appealing to Howard, given his obsession for streamlining and his previous experience with the construction of the Racer's wing.

The deal was completed on 24 July 1939. For $170,000, the Hughes Aircraft Division of the Hughes Tool Company obtained exclusive rights to use the Duramold process for the manufacture of large aircraft. The company also obtained the services of Virginius Clark, a well-known aeronautical engineer who had been responsible for developing Duramold.

Howard's Twin-Engined Fighter

Howard had already authorized his engineers to begin preliminary work on an advanced fighter-bomber, based on what he thought the military needed. Twice before he had failed to sell his designs to the Army. He had submitted his first one, a pursuit plane based on the Racer design, and known as the XP-2, in July 1935. The second design, for a twin-engined fighter, was submitted in a competitive bid in April 1937. Neither of them resulted in an order. Obsessed with a combination of perfection, ambition, and determination, he set out to build an airplane that would have such outstanding performance that the Army would have no grounds for refusing to buy it. To accomplish this, he quickly quadrupled the number of technical staff to be employed by Hughes Aircraft.

The D-2 under construction at the Hughes Aircraft plant in Culver City. (Florida Air Museum)

Burbank to Culver City

By the end of August 1939, the company had begun a full-scale program to develop a fighter-bomber, based on the Duramold process. Typically, Howard established the specifications without the knowledge or the blessing of the Army Air Corps.

To build the new airplane, Howard purchased 380 acres of land in Culver City and constructed a 60,000 square-foot, air-conditioned, humidity-controlled aircraft plant with an adjacent 9,000-foot runway. The entire Burbank operation was moved to the new plant and on the Fourth of July weekend of 1941, all the operations of Hughes Aircraft, until then located in Burbank, were moved to the new plant in Culver City.

Sherman Mills Fairchild was a pioneer in the fields of photography, aviation, and sound recording. Like Howard, he was a man of many talents and interests. He was also an entrepreneur who established a number of companies, some of which still bear his name.

Hughes D-2

Costly Secret

The Hughes Aircraft Company D-2 was a twin-engined, two-place, high performance aircraft. It was aerodynamically immaculate, with a pressurized cabin for high altitude work. The prototype was built in great secrecy, at a cost of more than $3,500,000.

No other aircraft manufacturer would have proceeded with such an advanced design to such a stage of its production, because the shareholders would have demanded more assurances and reviews of the design, before final construcion. But Howard Hughes did not have any shareholders, and his funding from the Hughes Tool Company, which he also owned outright, was, during the 1940s, unlimited. Hughes abandoned the design in favor of the D-5 after flight tests of the D-2 revealed the need for numerous design changes.

Problems with the D-2

When the D-2 was finished in May 1943, it was taken to Harper Lake, near Hinckley, California, where a hangar and other installations had been built to conduct a flight test program in secret, using the dry lake bed as a landing strip. As usual, Howard elected to act as his own test pilot and began flight testing on 20 June.

The airplane's flight characteristics were not good. The NACA Series 200 airfoil, chosen for its laminar flow wing, caused problems with the airplane's control surfaces, and this necessitated changes to the wing, ailerons, and flaps.

While this work was being undertaken, Howard and representatives from the Army Air Forces' Material Division at Wright Field began to discuss the development of a high-altitude photographic reconnaissance airplane, based on the D-2 design, which would be designated the D-5. To expedite its procurement, Hughes proposed to modify the existing D-2 by replacing its troublesome wings.

> "The ailerons were overbalanced and tended to go from one extreme position to the other and they had no aerodynamic balance whatsoever on them."
>
> —Howard Hughes describing problems with the D-2.

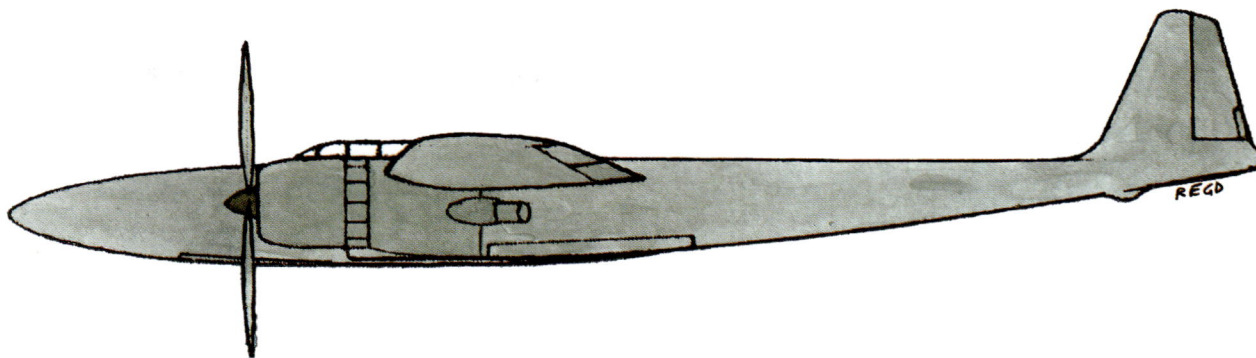

Howard Hughes's D-2 served as the prototype for the Army Air Forces's XF-11 (see page 60). The clean lines of this airplane emphasized Howard's preoccupation, amounting almost to an obsession, with aerodynamic perfection.

Length	34 ft
Wing Span	61 ft
Engine	Pratt & Whitney R-2800 (2,000 hp) x 2
Top Speed	433 mph
MGTOW	32,000 lb.

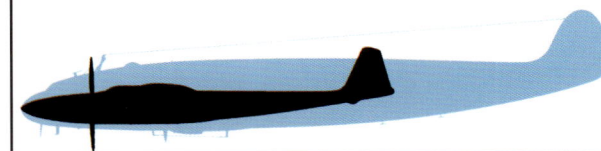

Size comparison with Constellation (p.55)

Because of the extreme secrecy under which the D-2 was built, few photographs of the finished airplane were ever taken. The picture shown above, taken at the Harper Lake test facility, is one of the only two photographs of the aircraft known to exist. The D-2 was the product of Howard's obsessive concentration on aerodynamic cleanliness. (Florida Air Museum)

The Kaiser-Hughes HK-1

Farewell to the D-2

Howard Hughes spent the next year negotiating with the USAAF until he finally received a letter of intent in mid-October 1943 to produce an entirely new aircraft, based on the D-5 design. Although the changes to the D-2's wings and control surfaces had corrected the most serious problems, the airplane was not considered a success, and was not flown again after Hughes flight-tested it for a second time on 2 August 1943. The wooden airplane remained in its air-conditioned, humidity controlled, wooden hangar until 11 November 1944, when it was destroyed by a mysterious fire and unexplained.

[There are those who think that Hughes wanted to get rid of the airplane and that the fire was not accidental. Howard did not like the airplane, and there is some evidence to suggest that he had tried earlier — during taxi tests on Harper Lake — to intentionally damage the D-2 beyond repair so that he could start over with a fresh design.]

Wartime Threat

In July 1942, the German submarine menace was sinking ships faster than the Allies could build them. **Henry J. Kaiser**, a one-time builder of roads and dams who had revolutionized the shipbuilding industry by mass-producing Liberty ships, proposed to build a fleet of giant flying boats to ferry men and supplies across the oceans.

The Kaiser-Hughes Partnership

Kaiser knew nothing about aviation, but after being rebuffed by Glenn Martin, he turned to Howard Hughes for help. For several days, Kaiser sought out Hughes, whom he had never met and knew only by his aviation fame. He finally located the reclusive millionaire, secluded in a hotel suite in San Francisco, where he had gone to recuperate from a bout with pneumonia.

Inspiration for a Giant Flying Boat

Kaiser's enthusiasm must have been contagious, for although Howard had serious reservations about the project, he agreed to team up with the loquacious industrialist, on condition that he had complete authority over the design. The next morning, newspapers across the country announced that Henry J. Kaiser and Howard Hughes had formed an alliance to build 500 giant airplanes in "the most ambitious aviation program the world has ever seen."

Construction Contract

The traditional aircraft industry considered the project to be a pipe dream and the military worried that it would divert men and materials from the war effort. Kaiser was backed by Hughes's reputation as an aircraft designer, however, and was able to convince the civilian authorities who were overseeing the production of war materiel to issue a letter of intent, dated 17 September 1942. This authorized the **Kaiser-Hughes Corporation** to proceed with the design and construction of three giant cargo-carrying flying boats that would be engineered "under the direction of Howard Hughes in his present plant at Culver City." Because there was a shortage of aluminum, Hughes and his engineers would build the aircraft out of Duramold.

Strict Contractual Conditions

Hughes Aircraft was prohibited from "stealing" engineers from other aircraft manufacturers engaged in war work, could not receive a fee or make a profit on the project, and was expected to deliver the airplanes in 24 months. This was an impossible set of conditions, especially the delivery time, and it was of great concern to Howard who was worried about what would happen to his reputation if he failed to deliver the airplane on schedule.

The Importance of a Name

The aircraft was designated either the HK-1, or the H-4 (Hughes No.4), or the Hercules. But never, at least within earshot of Howard, under pain of instant dismissal from the company, the journalist-inspired "Spruce Goose." As narrated on pages 69–75, this project was to be an important event in the history of airplane manufacture. It's construction was also to be the subject of a Congressional investigation, in which Howard displayed his command of technical details.

Henry J. Kaiser, an American industrialist, had reinvented methods of shipbuilding with the introduction of the Liberty ship in the Second World War. Refinements of the system of sub-assemblied components, the final assembly at the shipyard permitted rapid production. He was the master-mind behind the project to mass-produce flying boats. (Library of Congress)

The ill-fated D-2 parked in front of the air-conditioned, humidity controlled building at Harper's Lake that served as its hangar. (Florida Air Museum.)

Tragedy at Lake Mead

Solving a Problem

Toward the end of 1942, Howard flew the Sikorsky S-43 from Culver City and landed on the placid waters of Lake Mead, near Las Vegas, and 6,229 feet above sea level. In preparation for the HK-1 trials, he wanted to reduce the size of the step in the flying boat's hull to minimize the amount of drag it produced. Howard was convinced that by moving the step further back the center of gravity would be ahead of it. For hours at a stretch, he would taxi the S-43 on Lake Mead while speedboats trailed alongside, shooting hundreds of feet of film of the Sikorsky's hull as it glided through the water, seeking to understand the step's effect on the airplane's performance.

New Engines for the S-43

On one windless day, Howard attempted to take off, but the engines could not generate enough power at the lake's high elevation. He had to wait impatiently for the wind to pick up and a chop on the water to develop. Frustrated, he flew back to Culver City and ordered the 750-hp Pratt & Whitney engines to be replaced by 1,200-hp Wright R-1820s.

The change in engines, along with tail modifications, required new flight testing by the C.A.A. to provide an updated airworthiness certificate that was needed before the Sikorsky, which had been requisitioned by the Corps of Engineers, could be sold.

In the meantime, Howard continued with his personal test program. He flew the S-43 to Boulder City, not far from Las Vegas, where he maintained a permanent hotel suite. During a 4-month period, he made several hundred takeoffs and landings, none of which proved to be of much use, according to Gene Blandford (Howard's flight engineer).

C.A.A. Re-Certification

After months of shooting landings with the Sikorsky, Howard invited the C.A.A. to conduct his tests. The agency assigned Charles "Ted" Von Rosenberg, a C.A.A. test pilot, to the task, and the landings and takeoffs were completed in mid-May. All that remained were the water tests. Howard had insisted on going along on the flights as his own representative, and suggested that these should be conducted on Lake Mead. Monday, 17 May 1943, was chosen for the tests conducted out of the Boulder City Airport.

The day scheduled for the tests was bright and clear. As usual, Howard slipped into the pilot's seat on the left, leaving the right hand copilot's seat for Von Rosenberg. They were joined in the cabin by William M. "Ceco" Cline, a C.A.A. inspector; Gene Blandford, Howard's flight test engineer; and Richard Felt, a Hughes Aircraft mechanic. As they made ready for takeoff, Von Rosenberg asked Howard why he had not hired somebody else to do the testing. "Hell,"

he answered, "why should I pay somebody else to have all the fun?"

Tragedy

Howard took off and flew to the north end of the lake He liked to land the Sikorsky — which had notoriously poor handling characteristics in the water — fast and flat. This provided more rudder control and a smoother run-out. The weather was bright and clear as Howard touched down on the tranquil waters of the lake. As the amphibian began to settle in the water it pitched forward and started to go to the left. Howard added full right rudder and momentarily regained control. Then, without warning, the aircraft veered off course again. Before Howard could react, the Sikorsky swerved sideways, causing the right wing tip and float to dig into the water, tearing the wing apart. When the aircraft finally came to a stop it was steeply down by the nose, listing to the right at a 45° angle, and was rapidly filling with water.

Howard, who was momentarily dazed from a blow on the head, had to be pushed through the pilot's side window by Von Rosenberg, who made his own exit via the overhead escape hatch. Two of the other three crewmen aboard were not so lucky: Ceco Cline and Dick Felt were both killed in the crash.

The S-43 sits placidly on Lake Mead.
(courtesy: Dave Straub)

Wreckage of the S-43 being recovered from the lake.
(Florida Air Museum)

The S-43 after being rebuilt by Hughes.
(courtesy: Dave Straub)

Production Contract

High Performance for the Army Air Force

On 11 August 1943, Howard Hughes escorted **Colonel Elliott Roosevelt** (FDR's second son) on a tour of Hughes Aircraft in Culver City. Roosevelt, was then the chairman of a committee of battle-experienced photo-reconnaissance officers, and was leading a five-man team that was surveying potential production sites for a new high-performance photo-reconnaissance plane that was desperately needed by the Army Air Force. After touring the plant, Hughes accompanied them on the short flight to Harper Lake, where the D-2 was being secretly tested.

Roosevelt's team clustered around the impressive airplane, admiring its aerodynamically clean lines and its exquisitely smooth surface. While they were examining the D-2, a highly decorated Royal Air Force officer on Roosevelt's team told Hughes "I have never seen anything more magnificent that could do a better job."

Hughes D-2 to D-5

The enthusiastic reception given to the D-2 encouraged Howard to submit a proposal to the USAAF to supply 200 D-5 airplanes — an aircraft that was still in the planning stages, incorporating the all-wood Duramold fuselage of the D-2, with a metal wing and tail assembly. Although the Materiel Command at Wright Field, which was vehemently opposed to the use of wood, opposed the project, it was as enthusiastically endorsed by Colonel Roosevelt, who informed the chief of the Army Air Forces that "the D-5 was the only airplane already designed which is suitable for photographic purposes."

Hughes D-5 Contract

Six weeks later, on 11 October 1943, the aircraft division of Hughes Tool Company received a letter from the USAAF indicating that the U.S. Government would buy one-hundred D-5 airplanes, under a cost-plus fixed-fee contract, at an estimated cost of $48,555,000.00, exclusive of a fixed fee not to exceed four percent.

Howard the Thrifty

Negotiations on the formal contract were delayed by a controversy surrounding the development costs: Howard wanted to include the cost of the D-2; the USAAF did not. The impasse was not settled until 1 August 1944 when the USAAF agreed to apportion that part of the D-2's development cost that applied directly to the D-5, which was now designated the XF-11. Although the D-2 cost $3.5 million to design and build, only $1.9 million could be applied to the development of the XF-11.

XF-11 Cancellation

Development of XF-11 fell so far behind schedule that by VE (Victory in Europe) Day, 7 May 1945, it was no longer needed. Three weeks later, the USAAF canceled the 98-plane production portion of the XF-11 contract, leaving just the two prototypes for Hughes Aircraft to complete.

The Lockheed P-38 Lightning first flew on 27 January 1939. It was one example of twin-boom airplanes that were produced during the 1930s. Interestingly, Hughes Aircraft bid for the Air Forces contract, but lost out to Lockheed, much to Howard's chagrin.

Seen from any angle, the Hughes D-5 was a beautiful aircraft. With memories of previous disasters, the D-5's twin-boom design ensured good control through the two vertical stabilizers. Each piston engine on this, the beautiful XF-11 first prototype, shown here on the tarmac at Culver City in the spring of 1946, was equipped with two four-bladed contra-rotating propellers. (Florida Air Museum)

Hughes D-5 (XF-11)

XF-11

The XF-11 was a twin-boom, high-wing monoplane, designed for high-altitude photo-reconnaissance work. It was equipped with two sets of hydraulically-controlled contra-rotating propellers, manufactured by Hamilton Standard. The unique configuration — it had not been operationally tested before — would be the airplane's undoing and would have dire consequences for Howard Hughes

The aircraft's two-man crew, the pilot and relief pilot-navigator, were seated in a pressurized cockpit under a large Plexiglas canopy. The navigator could change places with the pilot during flight and could also perform the duties of photographer. The aircraft was designed to carry an impressive array of cameras mounted in the nose and in the rear of the left boom. Its performance characteristics — a ceiling above 40,000 feet and a top speed of 450 mph — were far superior to those of any reconnaissance aircraft then in service. The advent of the jet engine, however, hastened the obsolescence of all high-performance piston-engined aircraft, including the XF-11, which was never put into production.

Delays

Poor management — caused partly by Howard's continuing reluctance to delegate authority to others — and the lack of engineering expertise in metal airframe design, caused extensive delays in the development of the XF-11. By the time the first prototype was ready for flight testing in April 1946, the Second World War had ended in August 1945 and the aircraft was no longer needed. Although the USAAF had canceled the production portion of the contract a year earlier, it had left the prototype production portion intact for future research programs. Ground testing of the first prototype began on 15 April 1946, with Hughes at the controls. Readying the airplane for its first test flight took another two months. Experimental aircraft, such as the XF-11, ordered by the USAAF, were usually test-flown at the Army's flight test center (now called Edwards Air Force Base) near Muroc, California, in the Mojave Desert. But Howard had cajoled the Army brass into allowing him to act as his own test pilot for the initial test flights, to be flown from the airstrip at the Culver City plant. He scheduled the flight for Sunday, 7 July 1946.

Derived from Howard Hughes's D-2 (p.57) the XF-11 had contra-rotating propellers, more powerful engines, a plexiglass nose, and a redesigned cockpit.

Length	66 ft
Wing Span	101 ft
Engine	Pratt & Whitney R-4360 (3,000 hp) x 2
Top Speed	450 mph
MGTOW	58,300 lb.

Size comparison with Constellation (p.55)

The Air Force insignia varied slightly in the color arrangement during its formative years, but was eventually standardized, as shown below.

Howard Hughes warming up the XF-11's engines just before to the first test flight on 7 July 1946. (Florida Air Museum)

Near-Fatal Crash

High Speed Taxi Tests

Howard arrived at the Culver City plant early in the morning that Sunday and began a series of high-speed taxi tests to familiarize himself with the XF-11's ground handling characteristics. After each test run, the aircraft was returned to the hangar for further checking and testing. The mechanics worked on the airplane until late in the afternoon.

Howard Takes Off

Close to five o'clock, Howard finally pronounced the aircraft ready to fly, climbed into the cockpit, and taxied out to the runway, where he completed the last of his pre-flight check lists. At twenty minutes after the hour he pushed both throttles forward, roared down the grass runway, and took off into the clear California sky.

Assymetric Drag

Although the official test plan was limited to 45 minutes, Howard was still in the air an hour and fifteen minutes later, trying to figure out a problem with the landing gear — which according to the USAAF's test plan, should never have been retracted in the first place. The XF-11 suddenly yawed to the right and began to lose altitude.

The drag on the right side of the aircraft was so strong. Howard felt "as if someone had tied a barn door broadside onto the right hand wing." Unable to determine the cause of the problem, Howard unfastened his seat belt to get a better look at the right side of the aircraft. He still did not see anything wrong, "yet it felt as if some giant had the right wing of the airplane in his hand and was pushing it back."

Emergency Procedure

Howard returned to his seat and tried to increase the power on both engines, then cut back, and then increased the power again only on the right engine. Nothing worked. The XF-11 was losing altitude so fast that he had to find a place to land. Unable to make it back to the airstrip, he decided to try to make an emergency landing. The only open space he could see was the golf course belonging to the Los Angeles Country Club. He never made it.

Crash

The XF-11 was traveling at 155 mph when it struck the roof of a home at 803 North Linden Drive, in Beverly Hills. The aircraft sliced into the house next door, sheared off a utility pole, and finally came to rest in an alley. Howard crawled out of the cockpit and collapsed onto the burning wing before he was pulled to safety by a nearby bystander. He was lucky to be alive.

With Howard at the controls, the XF-11 takes off from the Culver City airstrip on its first flight. (Florida Air Museum)

The impact was so great that one of the engines, shown here, was thrown sixty feet through the air. The XF-11 initially struck the house shown at right, which was demolished in the resultant blaze.

Other parts of the airplane are scattered between the two damaged houses. Much of the wreckage was strewn throughout the backyard at 808 Whittier Street, Beverly Hills.

Fight For Life

Miraculous Survival

After being pulled from the wreckage, Howard was rushed to the emergency room of Beverly Hills Hospital. From there, the semi-conscious millionaire was taken by ambulance to Good Samaritan Hospital where he was treated by **Dr. Verne R. Mason**, his personal physician. His injuries were so severe that no one thought he would live through the night.

The crash nearly killed the 41-year-old test-pilot. It crushed his chest, fractured nine of his ribs on his left side and two on his right; displaced his heart to one side of his chest cavity; punctured a lung in six places, causing it to collapse; and severely burned his right hand. Less critical injuries sustained by Howard included second degree burns over his chest and buttocks, and a broken nose. He also suffered numerous cuts, bruises and abrasions over his entire body. Other than these injuries, he was apparently all right.

Amazing Recovery

At dawn Howard regained full consciousness and began the slow process of recovery. He would remain in the hospital for six weeks until 12 August 1946, when, against the advice of his physicians, he was released. He went home to his rented house in Beverly Hills, where his doctor arranged for 24-hour expert medical care. In the interim, the hospital was deluged with flowers, baskets of fruit, and get-well messages — including a telegram from President Truman — all addressed to Howard Hughes. The Twelfth Air Force even arranged to have a mass flight of aircraft circle the hospital. He was still a national hero.

Verdict

Howard had only one thing on his mind during the immediate aftermath of the crash: what had caused the drag on the right side of the XF-11 to cause it to crash? Even as he was being wheeled into Good Samaritan Hospital on the night of the accident, he was conscious enough to ask **Glen Odekirk** to find out what had caused the crash. Okekirk went to the crash site the next day and marked the propeller collars to show the blade setting before the wreckage was moved. He found that the right rear propeller was fourteen degrees in reverse pitch — evidence enough to indicate that the pitch change-measurement mechanism had failed.

'Lucky Hat'

A battered old dark gray felt hat that has been a symbol of his unbelievable good luck lies beside the bed on which Howard Hughes is struggling in a desperate fight against death today.

It is the same lucky hat that Hughes has always worn when he embarked on one of his air ventures...the same hat he was wearing when he crashed Sunday.

— *L.A. Herald Express*, 12 July 1946

Blow to an Ego

Weeks later, the official board investigating the accident found that the right rear propeller had lost oil, reversed pitch, and created excessive drag on the right side of the airplane. But the board, in a crushing blow to Howard's ego, concluded that a contributory cause of the crash was pilot error. Hughes was faulted for the way in which he had flown the aircraft and conducted the flight. The main allegation was that, before he took off, and even with his pre-flight inspections and check-list, there had been suspicions in the discrepancy in the oil consumed and in the contra-rotating propeller mechanism on the right side. But Howard had been too eager to fly that day and had taken a sadly miscalculated risk. He should also have kept to the 20-minute flight plan and stayed in closer contact with his ground staff and given reports.

Whether or not he admitted it to himself, Hughes was not the type to indulge in recriminations, and, as narrated on the next page, he did not waste time "crying over spilt milk" but continued with the flight-test program of the XF-11, almost as a matter of routine.

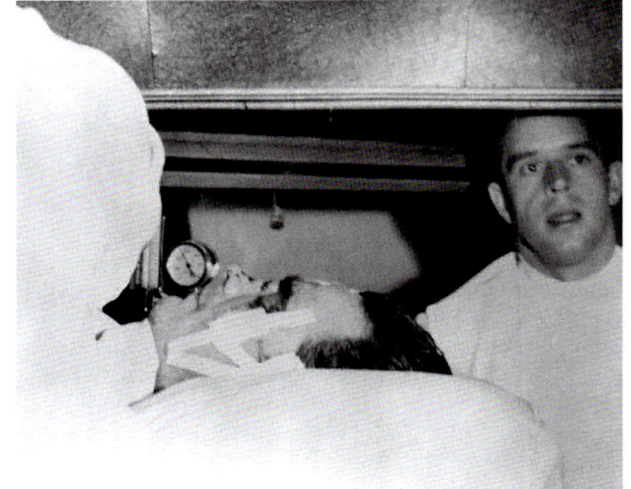

Critically injured in the crash of the XF-11, Howard Hughes is transported by ambulance to Good Samaritan Hospital in Los Angeles.

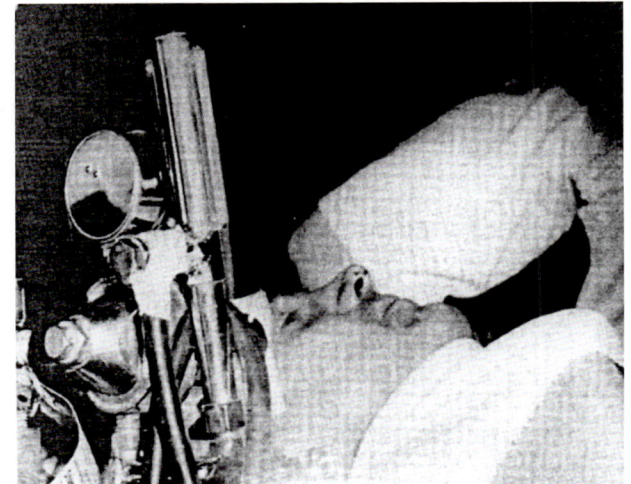

Another picture of Howard Hughes on his way to the hospital at a time when few of the ambulance men gave him much chance to live.

Resurrection of the Man

XF-11 Prospects

It is said that if you fall off a horse, you should get back on immediately to restore your confidence. Howard exercised this procedure *in excelsis*.

Howard Hughes never seemed to be the same again after his near-fatal crash. He grew a moustache to hide the scar on his upper lip. And there may have been other wounds that were never revealed, to say nothing of his life-long addition to pain killers.

In any case, while Howard was recuperating from the injuries suffered in the crash of the XF-11, the authorities at Wright Field asked Hughes Aircraft to "furnish the name of a test pilot, other than Mr. H.R. Hughes," who would test the second XF-11. Early in 1947 Howard flew to Washington to appeal personally against the decision not to let him fly the second XF-11. He promised to pay the government $5 million if the airplane crashed with him at the controls. Carl Spaatz, the new commanding general of the Air Force, had no objections to Hughes flying the airplane and issued the necessary orders permitting him to make the test flights.

Courageous Return

On 5 April 1947, nine months after his near-fatal crash, Hughes climbed into the second XF-11 and prepared the aircraft for takeoff. Noticeably absent from the aircraft were the counter-rotating propeller blades that had caused the accident that had nearly taken his life. In their place were standard four-blade propellers. The dramatic take-off was staged in front of some 500 Hughes Aircraft employees who had come out to watch their boss. Howard spent ninety minutes in the air over Culver City before landing. He emerged from the cockpit, smiling broadly, and was greeted by a round of applause from the spectators.

Before the Air Force would accept delivery of the XF-11, a number of test flights had to be flown to satisfy the terms of the government's contract. Most of these were conducted by Howard himself. He was very good at providing information on how the airplane felt and handled, but he was not a trained flight engineer. He was too much of an individualist and too undisciplined to provide the kind of data needed for quantitative analysis of the aircraft's performance characteristics.

Howard preparing to test the second XF-11. At least on this occasion, he had left his lucky hat behind. (Florida Air Museum)

The second XF-11 being prepared for flight. (Florida Air Museum)

The second XF-11 in flight. Note that the contra-rotating propellers (see page 61) have given way to conventional ones. (Florida Air Museum)

Undignified End to the XF-11

Howard had set himself a challenging goal, and no doubt in his own mind, he believed that he had fulfilled the obligations as set out in his contract with the customer. The Air Force formally accepted the XF-11 prototype in November 1947, conducting its own extensive flight test program in 1948. The full results of these have never been revealed. The aircraft was parked at Sheppard Air Force Base in Wichita Falls, Texas, to waste away until it was scrapped.

It was an undignified end for a truly distinctive and elegant example of visionary aircraft design.

Flying Again

"Getting Back on the Horse"

As mentioned in the previous page, Howard grew a moustache to hide the scar on his upper lip and there were undoubtedly psychological wounds that were never revealed, and which were to haunt him for the rest of his life.

As he grew stronger, Hughes worried that the accident might have made him apprehensive about flying. He had to prove to himself that he could still fly, not only for his own personal image of the daring aviator who had walked away from crashes, but also to dispel any doubts about his competence as a pilot. On 9 September 1946, photographers snapped pictures of Hughes at the controls of a Douglas B-23 Dragon that had been converted for private use by the Hughes Tool Company. He then took the airplane up on his first flight since the crash, and during the next few months, he flew everywhere — to New York, Kansas City, Dayton, and Mexico, this last for a needed vacation with Cary Grant.

Getting Away From It All

In January 1947, Howard took Cary, who was one of Howard's best friends and sidekick, on a flight in one of the converted B-23s. They flew east to New York, where Hughes had some business to do, and then headed west again. The flight plan called for a refueling stop in Amarillo, Texas. On their way back, Grant and Hughes disappeared in the midst of a raging thunderstorm that had grounded airplanes in six states. Across America, newspapers headlined the news that the famed aviator and handsome actor were missing and believed dead. Obituaries were rushed into type as executives of the Hughes Tool Company met in an emergency session to determine the legal implications of heirless ownership.

Off to Mexico

They were not aware that the two men, trying to avoid the inevitable and ever-present publicity, had intentionally disappeared, changing their flight plan so they could head for Mexico and a much-needed vacation from the press. They wanted it to be a secret so they pulled strings at various places to stop the news from getting out. The two men only became aware of the consternation over their assumed deaths after the maid servicing their Guadalajara hotel room became hysterical when she saw the two "ghosts" napping in their suite.

Business and Pleasure

Following the Second World War, Howard Hughes seems to have mixed business with pleasure; and with his wealth, he could, for the former, indulge in Big Business, and, for the latter, enjoy the company of the most attractive and beautiful women that Hollywood could create. Occasionally, he could take the business/pleasure relationship to a new level of sophistication, by requisitioning one of T.W.A.'s aircraft, even when it was ready for a scheduled service.

The Shady Tree Air Service

Lesser known was some of his little-known publicized private activities, based at the Hughes plant in Culver City. Normally, an airstrip or runway is cleared of all obstructions, but curiously, as the photograph shows, a clump of eucalyptus trees on the western edge of the strips seemed to survive the attentions of the bulldozers.

This was because this was the rendezvous for what a few privileged people who were "in the know" referred to as the Shady Tree Air Service. Howard and a select few of the staff would arrange their rendezvous with their lady friends, who would wait to be picked up at the Shady Tree by the Hughes private air service. The motley fleet usually comprised war-surplus B-23 bombers, but Howard's own Boeing 307 Stratoliner was known to make a pit-stop or two at the Shady Tree. Access from the adjacent road was through a gate. Howard had the only key.

The most frequent destination was Lake Tahoe, but Las Vegas, Reno, and other cities were on the non-scheduled and very unofficial map. On one occasion, the 307 was destined for Houston, but mistakenly landed at a nearby military base. The pilot was severely chastised by the base commander who at first did not know who he was talking to. In his usual "take charge" way, Howard (without money, as usual) claimed that he was low on fuel, and did not wish to risk a forced landing in a populated area, and could he borrow 50 gallons for each engine?

The long Culver City runway in 1947. The Shady Tree is half-way along on the right hand edge.

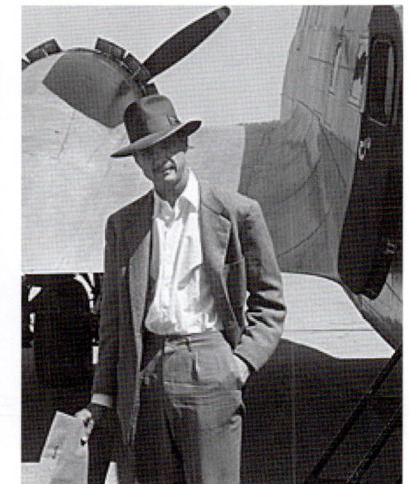

Howard Hughes in 1947.

Douglas B-23 Dragon

War-Surplus Bomber

The B-23 was a twin-engined bomber developed as a successor to the unimpressive Douglas B-18. First flown in July 1939, it incorporated many features of the Douglas DC-3 commercial transport. Although it was much faster than the B-18 and was the first operational Army bomber to be equipped with a tail gun, the Dragon was soon outclassed by more modern bombers such as the North American B-25 and the Martin B-26. Only 38 B-23s were built, none of which were used in combat during the Second World War, serving instead only in secondary roles as reconnaissance, training, transport, and test-bed aircraft. Twelve B-23s were converted as fast transports and redesigned UC-67s.

Executive Transport

After the war, all B-23s/UC-67s were declared surplus and many were sold to private operators for use as cargo and executive transports. At least five examples were purchased by the Hughes Tool Company and converted by the aircraft Division into executive transports. Howard favored the converted B-23s because of their speed, and used the airplanes frequently to fly back and forth between the east and west coasts.

HUGHES'S DOUGLAS B-23 FLEET

MSN	Serial No.	Reg'n	Remarks
2719	39-33	NC747	Delivered to Aberdeen proving ground, 21 May 40 for munitions testing. Sold to Hughes Tool Co. (as NC49548) on 2 June 1945 for $20,000, but sold immediately. Sold again to Hughes Aircraft, 6 Sept 48 for $25,000. Sold 21 Apr. 51.
2730	39-44	NC49811	Delivered 17 July 40. Sold to Hughes Tool Co., 28 Feb 45 for $20,000. Re-sold 1 Mar 49.
2732	39-46	NR53253	Delivered 18 July 40. Sold to Hughes Tool Co., 2 July 45 for $20,000. Sold 3 weeks later.
2746	39-60	NR44890	Delivered 20 Aug 40. Sold to Hughes Aircraft, 23 May 45 for $20,000. Licensed 1 Sept 45. Aircraft destroyed by fire 20 Oct 51.

(Fleet details, courtesy Matt Rodina)

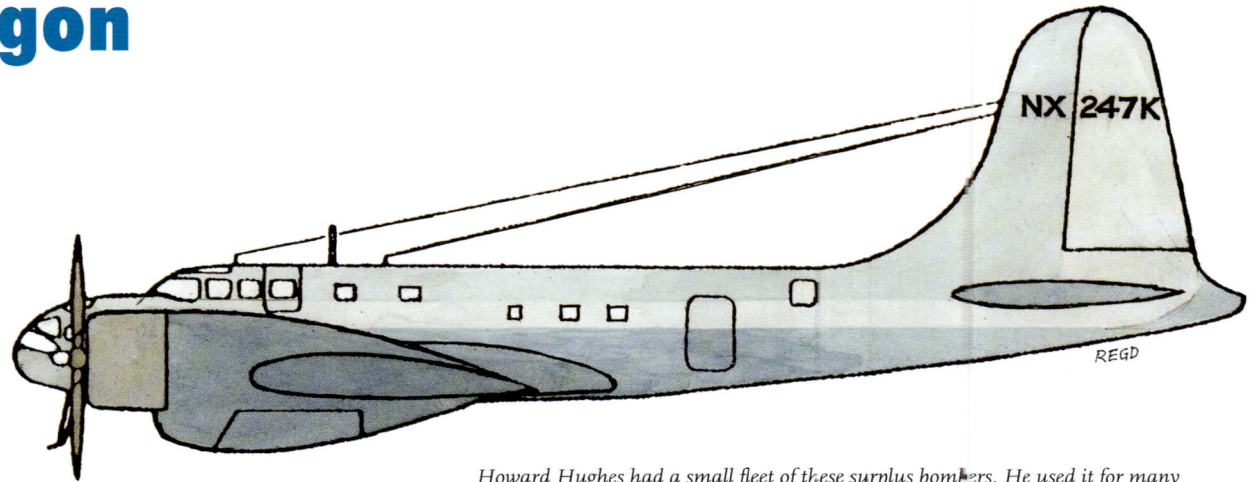

Howard Hughes had a small fleet of these surplus bombers. He used it for many pleasure flights while attending the notorious Congressional hearings before Senator Brewster.

Length	. . . . 58 ft
Wing Span	. . . . 92 ft
Engine	. . . . Wright R-2600-3 (690 hp) x 2
Seating	. . . . Crew 2, 6–10 passengers
Cruise Speed	. . . . .310 mph
MGTOW	. . . . .32,400 lb.
Max. Range	. . . . .2,750 miles

Size comparison with Constellation (p.55)

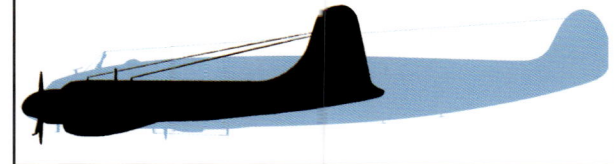

This rare photograph is of NR 44890, which may have been the flagship of the Shady Tree Air Service (see page 65).

Battle of the Atlantic

T.W.A. Across the Atlantic

In the spring of 1945, Howard and his airline had won a stunning victory over his arch-rival **Juan Trippe** and Pan American Airways, when the Civil Aeronautics Board awarded T.W.A. the right to fly across the North Atlantic. **Jack Frye**, T.W.A.'s president, cautioned Howard that he was moving into territory that had been Trippe's exclusive domain. As president of Pan American, "He is going to make your life miserable," warned Frye. That admonition came to pass a few months later, when **Owen Brewster**, known by the press as "Pan Am's spokesman in the Senate," was appointed chairman of the Senate War Investigating Committee, which was charged with scrutinizing defense contracts awarded during the Second World War (see next page).

Trans World Airlines

Howard Hughes never did things by halves. Like most of the U.S. domestic airlines, T.W.A. had contributed to the war effort with pilot training programs, maintenance bases, and military transport air service. When the Second World War ended, T.W.A. was among the airlines that were rewarded by international route certificates from the C.A.B. and approved by President Truman. T.W.A.'s wartime trans-Atlantic services with the Boeing Stratoliner were peacetime routes to Europe.

As early as 1946, Howard had the Constellations —the best in the business; he had the routes; and he changed the T.W.A. name neatly from Transcontinental & Western Air to Trans World Airlines, thus keeping the same initials. His certificated route pattern stretched as far east as Cairo and India. Undoubtedly he must now have cherished the idea of challenging the Pan American Airways previously-held monopoly of overseas routes.

Round the World Ambitions

T.W.A felt its way into South America by buying an interest in the Central American airline, TACA. During the early postwar years also, the airline acquired financial interests in, or acted in advisory capacity, to many other airlines around the world, just as before, Pan Am had secured footholds in the Americas and in China. Whether or not the ambition was of a round-the-world airline empire, by the late 1960s, T.W.A. had become the biggest airline on the North Atlantic.

The Mighty Fallen

But the TransWorld name was never backed by TransWorld achievement. A close association with Northwest Airlines to form (what would now be called a code-sharing agreement) around-the-world air service; and a later attempt to launch a trans-Pacific route, both failed to materialize. Like his great Pan Am adversary, Juan Trippe, Howard Hughes did not live to see his airline, under a management from which he had been completely divorced, go into Chapter 11 bankruptcy and eventually disappear from the airline record books.

After the end of the Second World War, Pan American Airways lost its monopoly of United States international air routes. T.W.A. was one of the major beneficiaries. In January 1946, the words "TransWorld" appeared on the timetables, although the name, Transcontinental & Western Air was not officially changed until 17 May 1950. Trans-Atlantic service began February 1946 with a route from Washington and New York to Paris, via Gander and Shannon. An extension to Cairo was made two months later and a route to Lisbon and Madrid started in May. By 1947, T.W.A. was serving India at Bombay, and extended his route to Colombo in the summer of 1953. Ambitions to create a round-the-world service subsided and Hughes's airline reached only as far east as Manila in 1957.

Airline	Date of Initial Interest	Details of Affiliation
TACA (Panama)	5 Oct 43	T.W.A. share 22%. Reduced in Feb 49. Sold to Waterman Steamship Company, 1951.
Aerovias Brazil	5 Oct 43	Acquired with TACA which controlled T.W.A. Interest reduced to 9%, 11 Jan 47, to Brazilian investors. T.W.A. interest withdrawn 1950.
British West Indian Airways (B.W.I.A.)	5 Oct 43	Acquired TACA. T.W.A. interest reduced in 1947, and sold to Trinidad Government in 1952.
Philippine Air Lines	Aug 45	Agreement, 1944. T.W.A. shareholding 40%, 10 Jan 46. Reduced to 2%, March 1968.
Hawaiian Airlines	May 44	T.W.A. purchased 20% stock. Sold in 1948.
Technical & Aero. Exploitation Co. (T.A.E.) (Greece)	6 Apr 46	T.W.A. shareholding 35%, reduced to 15%, July 51. Shares sold to Aristotle Onassis, 1 Jan 57.
Ethipian Airlines	26 Dec 45	Technical and management assistance. No financial interest. Gradually withdrawn.
Saudi Arabian Airlines	20 Sep 46	Technical and management assistance. No financial interest. Arrangement lasted for almost 40 years.
Linee Aeree Italiane (L.A.I)	16 Sep 46	Co. established w/40% T.W.A. shareholding. Reduced to 30% in 1952. Withdrawn when L.A.I. merged with Alitalia 1 Sep 1957.
Iranian Airways	26 Oct 46	Co. formed with 10% T.W.A. shareholding and management contract. Withdrawn when Iranian Goverment reorganized airline in 1949.
Trans Mediterranean Airways (T.M.A.) (Lebanon)	4 Aug 64	Organized engine overhaul shop. Technical management contract, 12 November 1966

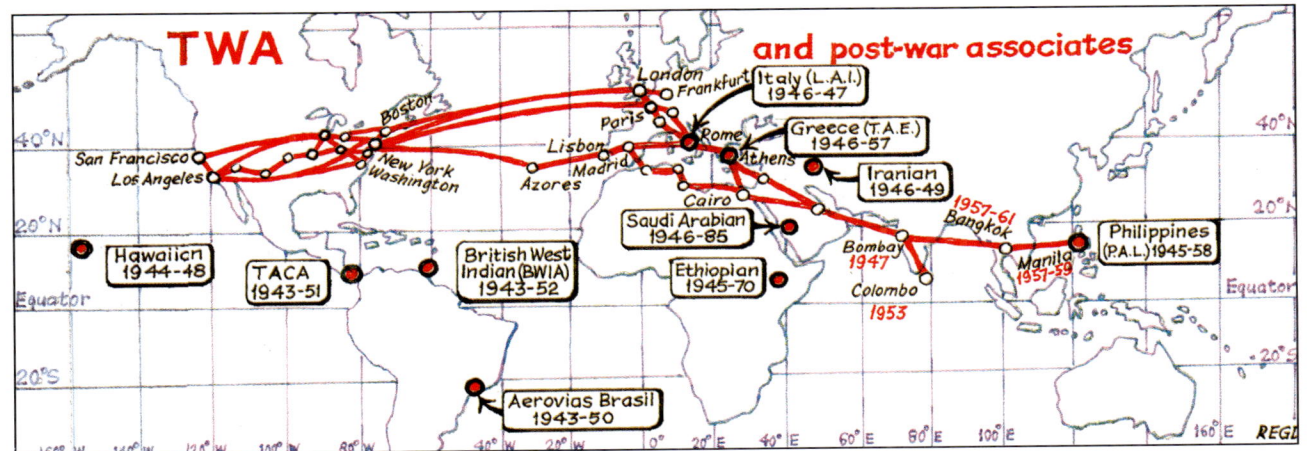

TWA and post-war associates

Saving the HK-1

In the Balance

The flying boat project continued to limp along until February 1943, when the chairman of the War Production Board, **Donald M. Nelson**, finally decided to cancel the Defense Plant Corporation contract that had authorized the Kaiser-Hughes Corporation to build three flying boats for $18 million. Telegrams advising the company to stop work were soon on their way. Neither Hughes's showmanship, nor Kaiser's connections, were enough to save the flying boat. For that, Howard would have to rely on the help of **Jesse H. Jones**, a family friend and fellow Texan who was Secretary of Commerce and Federal Loan Administrator — two powerful positions within the administration that gave him tremendous control over how the government's money for war materials was spent.

Jones wielded so much power and influence in Washington that the press had dubbed him the "fourth branch of government." Among his decisions had been to assure C.R. Smith, of American Airlines, enough financial guarantee support to launch the Douglas DST (Douglas Sleeper Transport), developed from the original DC-1 and DC-2s, in which Howard had been involved. It was a classic case of "not what you know, but who you know."

Hughes Goes It Alone

Jones quietly intervened with **President Roosevelt** who was easily convinced that the millions of dollars already spent on the project would be wasted if the prototype was not completed. On 17 March 1943, the Defense Plant Corporation informed Hughes that it was canceling the original contract issued to the Kaiser-Hughes Corporation but issuing a new contract to the Hughes Tool Company to build a single airplane for the same amount of money called for in the original contract.

Nevertheless, to complete the HK-1, which had already cost $13 million and was only half finished, Hughes would have to spend millions of dollars of his own money. No other aircraft manufacturer in the world (except possibly the state-subsidized industry of the Soviet Union) could have undertaken such a vast project and under such demanding terms.

Keeping Busy

By this time, Howard had apparently decided that he had to leave because he had other problems. The designers, engineers, and project managers would do the work on this vast undertaking, but without his interfering micro-managing. This, one of the greatest episodes in the history of aircraft construction, was only part of Hughes's life. He was still the owner of T.W.A., a great airline and possibly with a more ambitious future; and he was still making a habit of partnering beautiful women, with whom he was able to spend a lot of days and nights. During the 1940s, Howard Hughes was far from idle.

Early in 1943, when the fate of the Hercules was in the balance, it was still only half finished. (Chal Bowen collection)

Donald M. Nelson, the highly influential chairman of the War Production Board (W.P.B.) had the final say on whether or not the original Hercules contract should be cancelled.

Left to Right: Howard Hughes standing next to Jesse H. Jones, family friend and fellow Texan who interceded with FDR to save the flying boat contract. (Library of Congress)

Resurrection of a Plan

A Hint of Trouble

In the spring of 1943, the civilian inspectors who had been overseeing the huge flying boat project began to concede that the engineering staff that Hughes had assembled had neither the executive nor the practical experience to run a project of such magnitude. Engineering was way behind schedule, none of the major assembly jigs had been built, and vast sums of money had been wasted. Howard's inability to relinquish control of any part of the project's design contributed to the delays. "He would spend all night worrying about the minutest details that any young engineer was quite capable of handling," explained **Dick Morrow**, an aerodynamics specialist who worked on the project. "He [Howard] insisted on digging into details way beyond what he should."

The Wood Problem

An even bigger threat to the project was the idea — first broached by **Grover Loening** on 3 April — that it was no longer necessary to construct the giant airplane out of wood. Loening, who was the aviation advisor to the War Production Board (W.P.B.), wanted the flying boat's wing to be built of aluminum, for which there was no longer a shortage. Howard refused to switch materials, fearing — probably correctly — that a change to metal construction would cause additional delays that would ultimately lead to the project's cancellation.

Late in September 1943, Loening went to the Hughes plant in Culver City to investigate the progress being made on the design of the giant flying boat that was to be named the Hercules. By then, Howard had taken steps to improve the management team responsible for its production. However, Loening's report was not favorable. In addition to his concerns over the use of wood, he had serious doubts about the design, which was seriously over-weight, and of its usefulness because the submarine threat was now greatly diminished. By this time, shipping troops by sea was not as dangerous as it was in previous years. Loening's report triggered an investigation by the W.P.B.'s Air Production Board, which concluded that the Hercules was no longer needed. Before canceling the project however, Henry Kaiser and Howard Hughes were invited to appear before the Board to answer questions on the technical merits of the project and its value to the war effort.

Contract Deferred

Both men journeyed to Washington to defend their project. Hughes argued that the knowledge to be gained justified the cost of going forward. After three days of futile discussions, he and Kaiser arranged a private meeting with the Executive Vice-chairman of the W.P.B., **Charles E. Wilson**. This was a classic case of "if you want something done, go to the top." Two top men, one in aviation and both went to the top. They held some strong industry cards and convinced Wilson to defer canceling the project until it could be reappraised from an engineering standpoint.

The Consolidated Coronado

No doubt in preparation for his investment in the huge HK-1 flying boat, Howard bought a Consolidated PB2Y Coronado, a large flying boat formerly in service with the United States Navy, and flown by Pan American Airways on its behalf over the Pacific Ocean. But he never flew the aircraft, and it was laid up in Long Beach Harbor until it was dismantled.

(Left) The wind tunnel model used for NACA testing. The HK-1 was one of the most aerodynamically clean fuselages ever tested. It probably had the lowest drag coefficient for any flying boat ever built.

(Right) The hull of the wind-tunnel takes shape using wooden formers. "Taking shape" was a good description as it was a very good shape. Such was the magnitude of the ambitious project, even the model was bigger than many other aircraft which were themselves considered to be large.

Building the HK-1 Hercules

The vast interior of the huge hangar in which the wing of the HK-1 Hercules was built. (Chal Bowen collection)

The twin hangars at Culver City dwarfed the Hughes Aircraft's previous assembly buildings. (Chal Bowen collection)

The wing of the HK-1 was 320 feet long, or the length of a football field (or the 100 meters dash). Developing the glue for the Duramold process took two years. (Chal Bowen collection)

A large crane moves one of the sub-assemblies — very carefully. The scale can be judged by the size of the men in the photograph. And this was only a wing flap. (Chal Bowen collection)

Battle in Washington

Senate Investigation

On 12 February 1947, in its first session under Republican leadership, Owen Brewster announced that his Senate War Investigating Committee or the Special Senate Committee, would begin to investigate the airplane contracts that Hughes Aircraft had received to construct the XF-11 and the Hercules flying boat, neither of which had yet been accepted by the government. Before the hearings began, Brewster charged Hughes with every kind of possible impropriety in his dealings with the government—creating a case against Hughes before Howard had a chance to speak for himself publicly. But he did respond to Brewster's blistering attacks with a series of newspapers articles that appeared across the nation, calling upon the Senator to "tell the whole truth" about the investigation and the efforts to prevent T.W.A. from competing with Pan American.

The Hearings Begin

The hearings into the Hughes contracts opened in Washington on 18 July 1947. They dragged on over several days, and led by Senate Brewster, established a substantial case, not to mention a character assassination, against a man who had once had a ticket tape parade down Broadway. However, they under-estimated their anticipated victim. Misled by his reputation as a rich playboy and self-seeking headline-maker, they should have done their homework. For Howard was no fool.

Witness for the Defence

On 6 August, as the last witness to be called, Howard Hughes took the stand. His testimony was extensive. Howard had a prodigious memory which he put to good use. Recalling dates, dollar amounts, specific provisions of his contracts, and other minute details about the operation of Hughes Aircraft, he conveyed the impression of a man who had always kept his finger on the pulse of his company at all times. For four days Howard thoroughly enjoyed himself as he outflanked, second-guessed, and completely unsettled the committee. In an outgoing and extrovert performance that was uncharacteristic of the multi-millionaire flyer, who was not noted for flamboyance of this kind, it was a masterpiece of sustained oratory.

He shrewdly identified a chink in his opponents' armor of criticism. Instead of exploiting Howard's greatest weakness: poor management of his government contracts, the committee spent hours grilling Hughes in a futile effort to establish that he was a wartime profiteer. The facts revealed just the opposite. He had lost millions of dollars trying to become a major aircraft manufacturer.

When the senators criticized the flying boat, Howard rallied to the defense of the Hercules. The airplane was never meant "to haul excursion passengers from Coney Island..." he replied sarcastically, explaining that it could be used only "for testing and research." He explained:

"I have put the sweat of my life into this thing, my reputation is wrapped up in it. I have stated that if it fails, I will leave the country, and I mean it."

Senator Owen Brewster (left) and Howard Hughes (right) on 11 February 1947 after the secret meeting held at Howard's request to discuss his wartime contracts informally with the committee. (Library of Congress)]

Exit Brewster

After five days of "the sideshow to end all sideshows," wrote Richard Hack in his definitive biography of "America's first billionaire," the Special Senate Committee had learned little more than the maximum number of spectators who could fit into its caucus chambers.

On the sixth day, the subcommittee's chairman called the committee to order just long enough to call for an adjournment that was never resumed.

"I thought this investigation would drag my reputation through the mud," Howard told the reporters. But the "American public believes in fair play and because they supported me, I have more friends now than I ever had in my life."

Senator Brewster, an aggressive politician, lost much respect, and was a spent force.

Howard Hughes had good reason to appear self-satisfied after his victorious debate before the Special Senate Committee.

The Launching

Culver City to Long Beach

Confused contractual arrangements, the lack of a priority for materials, and the red tape that resulted from the Kaiser-Hughes set-up: all these caused innumerable delays to the HK-1, which remained unfinished until after the war had ended. As the giant flying boat neared completion in the spring of 1946, the Reconstruction Finance Corporation, which had issued the contract to build the HK-1, was anxious to move the nearly-finished aircraft from Culver City so that the Government-owned plant in which it had been constructed could be sold. After careful investigation, Howard leased a site on Terminal Island in Long Beach Harbor that would be used for the final assembly and checkout point.

Flying Boat Take-off Problem

On 11 June 1946 large sections of the aircraft (the entire hull, wings, empennage, flaps, etc.) all of which had been constructed at the Hughes Aircraft plant at Culver City, were transported to Long Beach, near to the Harbor, where they were to be assembled in a special graving dock that had been built to accommodate the gigantic seaplane. Moving the components 28 miles took two days to accomplish. The largest piece of the ship was the 200-ft long hull, which was 30 feet high, 24 feet wide, and weighed 122,000 pounds (60 tons). It was transported on a specially constructed trailer, which had ten sets of wheeled dollies.

Final Assembly

During the Senate hearings early in the following year (see following page) Brewster mocked the flying boat, calling it a "flying lumberyard" that would never fly. "I don't build cluck airplanes." Howard told a reporter. Now he set out to prove it. The total cost of the entire operation will never be known. Preparation of the dry dock at Long Beach alone took a year to complete.

When he returned to Los Angeles, he had but one thought: to fly the Hercules. In Long Beach, the job of assembling the giant flying boat was almost completed. Its giant wings, tail, and stabilizers were in place, and workers were just finishing the job of hooking up miles of wires, ducts, and tubing. On 25 October 1947, Hughes announced that he would conduct taxi tests during the next weekend.

Some idea of the size of the HK-1 can be gleaned from this picture of the enormous wing, under construction.

The fuselage emerges from its hangar at Culver City.

The HK-1 in its dry dock, ready for final assembly. The earth still had to be removed for the launching.

After the earth in front of the HK-1 was removed, the dry dock was filled with water and the giant flying boat was eased into Long Beach Harbor.

The Hughes Hercules photographed during its taxi tests. (Chal Bowen)

The Flight

Preparations

Howard did not mention of a plan to actually fly the ship, but he fully intended to take it into the air. That week — meticulous as usual — he flew the rebuilt Sikorsky S-43 to a remote stretch of the Colorado River, where he made 126 practice landings to sharpen his skills in flying off and on water.

On Saturday, 1 November 1947, Howard arrived at Long Beach's Terminal Island to take charge of floating the giant flying boat out of its dock and mooring it in Long Beach Channel. This delicate operation took most of the day to accomplish. He was the man in charge, as is depicted by photographs of him standing on top of the HK-1 as it is gently guided down the slipway into the water.

He returned the next morning for the taxi tests, briefly visiting the press tent before boarding the Hercules. Public relations man **Johnny Meyers** created a media event that would outshine the *Hell's Angels* premier. More than 500 reporters, photographers, and newsreel people were on hand the next day when the taxi tests were scheduled to begin.

Taxi Tests

At midday, the press were on board for the maiden taxi test — a three-mile run up the bay and back. Howard cautioned them not to expect too much. "We'll reach speeds of only about 40 mph," he said. Then he clambered up the ladder to his topside vantage point to supervise the positioning of the two sea mules used for towing.

When they arrived at the test area, Hughes and his flight engineers started the eight engines one by one until in a dramatic, almost theatrical, debut, all eight propellers whirled and glistened in the sunlight.

Will He or Won't He?

In a series of three short taxi runs, Hughes accelerated to about 40 knots and then decelerated as he felt out the airplane's performance, then turned around and began the second run, heading back to where they had started. This time the Hercules reached seventy-five knots before Howard closed the throttles and brought the flying boat to a stop, allowing the airplane to weathercock into the wind, its engines idling.

"Will you fly the boat today?" a reporter asked.

"Of course not." Howard replied.

"In that case," said the reporter, "is there a possibility of going ashore to file my story." Howard obliged by calling a boat to pick up the reporter. None of the other reporters wanted to be "scooped," and this triggered an exodus of newsmen. Only seven or eight reporters and a couple of photographers elected to stay aboard, including **James C. McNamara** of radio station KLAC, the only radio newsman aboard.

The Controversial Flight

With only his crew and the few newsmen who chose to remain aboard, Hughes began what had been billed as the

final taxi run of the day. Turning to one of his flight engineers, **David Grant**, he instructed "lower fifteen degrees of flaps," then turned the Hercules into the wind and advanced the throttles once again. Slowly gathering speed in the face of blustery wind, the huge flying boat sliced through the water, smoothly rose onto its step, and then effortlessly lifted off the water as soon as they passed 70 mph.

The big ship flew for about a mile before Hughes set it down, gently and without incident. The unexpected liftoff caught everyone ashore by surprise. A gasp and then a cheer went up from the thousands lining the harbor. Small pleasure boats, gathered to watch the tests, tooted their horns.

"Give Me All You've Got"

In the cockpit, Hughes was like a "little kid," recalled Joe Petrali, one of his crewmen. "He was grinning, and talking a lot...." His flight engineer, **Chalmer Bowen**, in charge of the engine settings, had guessed Howard's intention by the way he had spent several hours checking everything. At the vital moment, Howard had instructed "give me all you've got," and later, Howard gave Chal Bowen a broad wink as he stepped back out of the flying deck.

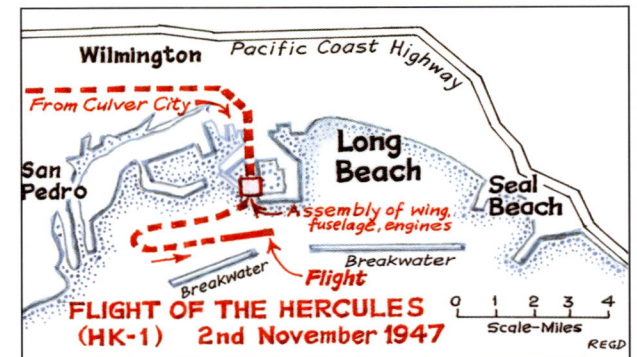

The HK-1 did not fly very far, only about 1 mile and from the relatively calm waters of Long Beach Harbor. But it achieved Howard Hughes's objective: he proved that his giant flying boat could fly. The HK-1 remained at Long Beach, protected in its air conditioned and climate-controlled hangar until it was finally sold and transferred to the museum at McMinnville, Oregon in 1993.

The Hughes HK-1 or H-4

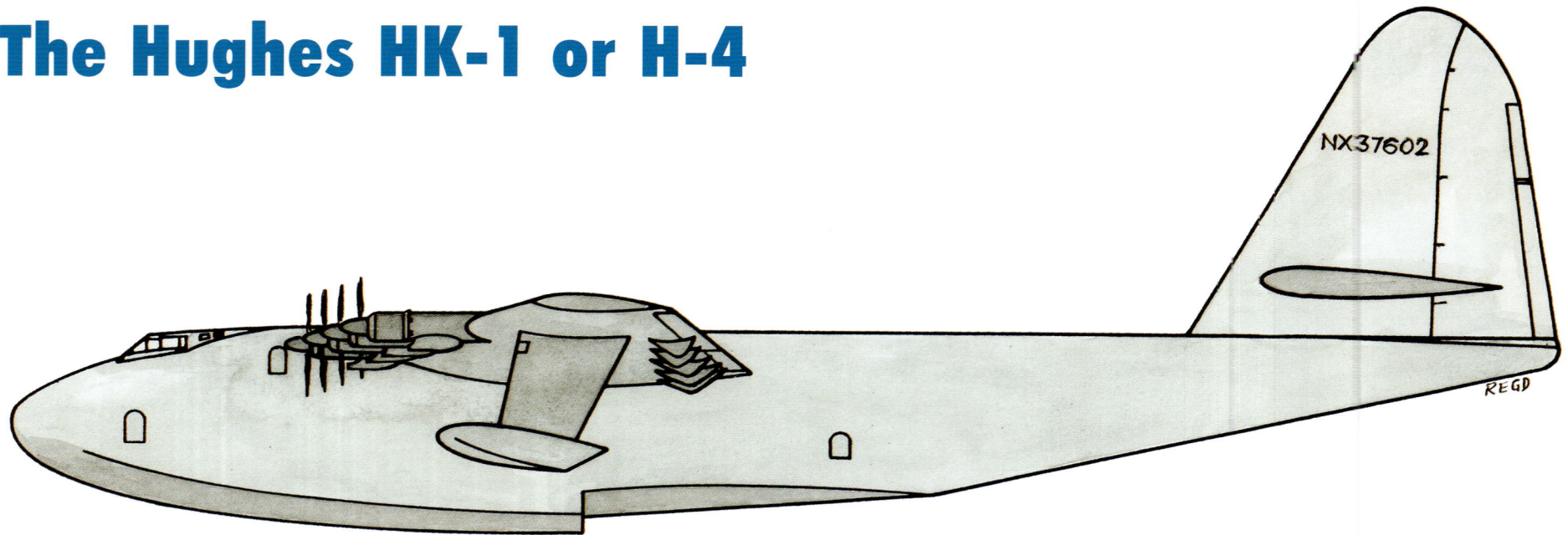

NX37602

REGD

Howard Hughes's enormous flying boat was anything but ungainly — as some giant airplanes have been in the past. Its classic lines were those in the best flying boat tradition. The use of the Duramold laminated wood construction ensured aerodynamic cleanliness, with few surface protuberances. Its eight engines were enough to lift it off the water in Long Beach Harbor but there is much doubt as to whether the HK-1 Hercules could have flown over a long range and certainly not with the payload of a battalion of soldiers, for which it was designed.

The Hughes-Kaiser HK-1 (Hughes H-4, or Hercules) was built to carry seven hundred passengers or a load of sixty tons. It was twice as big as any other aircraft of its day. For two decades it held the record as the largest aircraft in the world and still remains as the largest propeller-driven aircraft ever built. Although it no longer holds the record of the biggest in terms of lifting capacity, it still has the largest wing span of any aircraft ever built. The massive 200-ton aircraft, now in the museum at McMinnville, Oregon, is also the largest wooden airplane in the world, having been constructed almost entirely of birch laminations, molded into formers, using the Duramold process.

The specification for the giant flying boat includes one statistic that has never been exceeded. The wingspan of the HK-1, at 320 feet — longer than a football field — is still a record.

Length	219 ft
Wing Span	320 ft
Engine	Pratt & Whitney R-4360 (3,000 hp) x 8
Top Speed	235.5 mph
MGTOW	400,000 lb.
Max. Range	2,975 miles

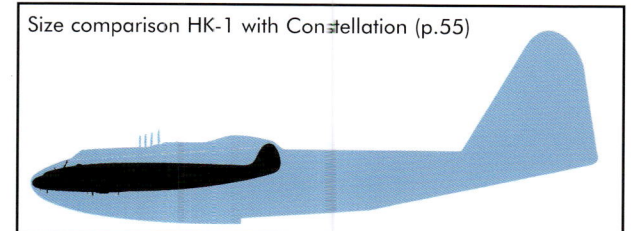

Size comparison HK-1 with Constellation (p.55)

The World's Biggest Aircraft

Howard surveys the flight deck before the epochal flight.

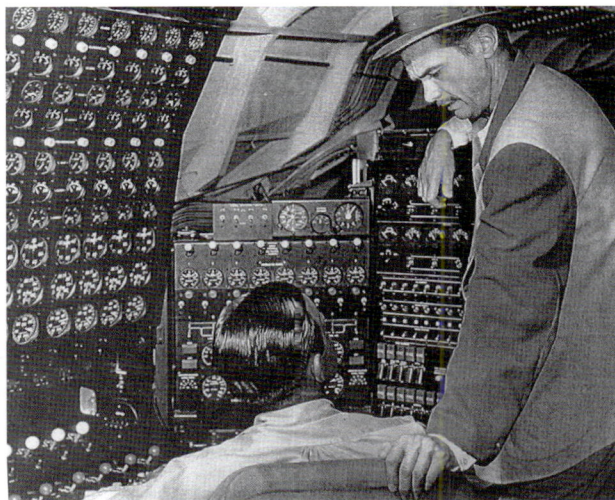

Howard checks all the instruments of the eight engines with Chalmer Bowen, his flight engineer. (Chal Bowen collection)

A Place in History
The ultimate career that was intended for the HK-1 will never be known. With more powerful engines, it might have been able to carry a battalion of infantrymen, or even armoured cars and tanks, across the oceans.

Length 177 ft., Span 230 ft., all-up weight 145 tons, Speed 330 mph
Overlapping the period while Howard Hughes was building the Hercules, the Bristol Aeroplane Company in England was building the Type 167 Brabazon. Construction began in October 1945, but it was underpowered, and a second airplane, with Proteus engines, never flew. A short-haul version for B.E.A. could have carried 180 passengers. It had too many technical problems and was scrapped in 1953.

Length 219 ft., Span 320 ft., all-up weight 200 tons, Speed 200 mph
The HK-1's wing span was the longest ever built. It was built entirely of Duramold, a resin-impregnated laminated wood material. It made one flight, of about 1 mile. Until the Soviet Antonov An-124, ancestor of the giant An-225, illustrated below, it was the heaviest airplane ever built.

Length 276 ft., Span 290 ft., all-up weight 600 tons, Speed 500 mph
The 1988 6-engined Antonov An-225, the Mriya, is the world's largest aircraft. Fully loaded, it can carry 250 tons of freight, or (as it was designed for), to carry the Soviet Space Shuttle, Buran. Only two were built.

A comparison with other large aircraft, past, present, and future, is interesting. The HK-1 took its place among several large aircraft that were visualized as the shape of Things to Come. Until the beginning of the 21st Century, none went into series production. Finally, however, the time of the giant commercial airliner has arrived, with the Airbus A380, depicted on this page.

Length 131 feet, Span 157 feet, all-up weight 60 tons, Speed 90 mph
On one occasion, the 12-engined Dornier Do X of 1929 carried 169 people on a short flight; but its round-trip Atlantic tour during 1930–1932 was punctuated by many delays. Four of these aircraft were built.

Length 239 ft., Span 262 ft., all-up weight 617 tons, Speed 600 mph
The Airbus A380 is the European Consortium's bold venture to establish a new generation of "Super-Jumbo-Jets" to succeed the veteran Boeing 747s. It has two passenger decks to carry 550 people in mixed class, or up to more than 800 in all-economy class. It is in full production and will go into service at the end of 2006. This picture emphasizes its size.

Into the Missile Age

New Interests

Toward the end of the Second World War, the Air Force began to award development contracts for a variety of guided missiles. Because the major airframe manufacturers were overloaded with war work, many of these contracts were awarded to the smaller manufacturers such as Hughes Aircraft. In January 1945 Hughes was awarded an Air Force contract to develop the airframe of an experimental air-to-air missile designated the JB-3. Named the **Tiamat**, this was a solid-fueled, rocket-propelled, air-to-air missile, guided to its target by a radar-homing seeker. It was designed to carry a 100-lb warhead at 600 mph at altitudes up to 50,000 feet.

First Terrain Avoidance Radar

The project introduced Hughes Aircraft to the radar equipment developed during the Second World War. By 1947, a small team of engineers was assigned to the electronics department, which, headed by **David Evans**, installed the first terrain avoidance radar system to be used on a civil airliner. Officially known as the Terrain Warning Indicator (TWI), it warned the pilot when within 2,000 feet of a hill or a mountain, activating an alarm in the cockpit. Adapted from a wartime tail-warning radar, it projected a radar beam behind the bomber to detect an enemy aircraft approaching from the rear. Howard was intrigued enough to buy the equipment from the Air Force, and with the help of his own engineers, changed the antenna to point downwards instead of straight back.

Raising Hair

The system weighed only 16 lb. and was installed on a Constellation. It was demonstrated to the press during three hair-raising flights from Culver City, carried out in the early part of May 1947. Supremely confident, Howard conducted the flights personally and was at the controls as the airplane flew at low altitude into the canyons surrounding Los Angeles. He headed directly for the menacing cliffs until the alarm sounded at the 2,000-foot warning level. With less than five seconds to spare, he would ram the throttles full forward, making an abrupt steep climbing turn as he just barely cleared the canyon walls.

Mr. Hughes' statement follows:

"This radar instrument warns the pilot (by a brilliant red light and a warning horn) the instant the airplane comes too close to the ground or any building, bridge, mountain, airplane, or other obstacle, regardless of darkness or weather conditions.

"I believe it will be of great assistance in our efforts to eliminate the type of accident which received so much publicity last year.

"For that reason, I am now installing this equipment on all TWA airplanes, and I intend to make it available as soon as possible, without profit, to all airlines throughout the United States."

Howard Hughes in the cockpit of a Constellation in which the new Terrain Warning Indicator System has been installed. The radar warning system — the four lights shown in the center of the instrument panel just below the windshield —indicates when the aircraft is approaching an obstacle. (Library of Congress)

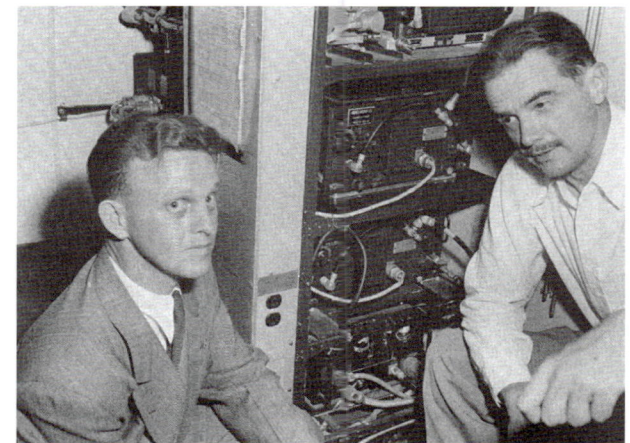

The JB-3 Tiamat was an experimental project started during the Second World War to produce a radar guided air-to-air missile. (USAF)

Howard discussing the installation of the Terrain Warning Indicator radar system with Dave Evans, head of the Electronics Department, Hughes Aircraft.

From Aeronautics to Avionics

Bell Labs of the West

Early in 1947, Howard Hughes met General Ira C. Eaker, the retiring chief of the Army Air Forces, to persuade him to take the position of vice president with the Hughes Tool Company. Howard believed that the armed services were going to have difficulty getting money for research and development, and he asked for Eaker's help in establishing an electronics laboratory that would be vital to national security. "I think we are going to be in trouble again," he told Eaker, "and the side that has the best weapons this time will win."

Falcon

The contract for the JB-3 guided missile awarded to Hughes Aircraft at the beginning of 1945 was destined to be short-lived. The program to develop a complete missile was terminated in June 1947 for budgetary reasons and the project was limited to the development of a radar target-seeker with a two-mile range and a fire control system applicable for a supersonic air-to-air missile. The project was revised again in March 1948 when the contract was modified to include the development of the MX-904 missile, which was later named the Falcon.

The study and development of the electronic control and guidance system for this missile allowed Howard to begin to assemble the personnel that would form the nucleus of the world-class electronics laboratory that he had discussed with General Eaker. Among the first specialists to be recruited were Simon Ramo and Dean Wooldrige, two outstanding scientists who would later found TRW, one of the most important aerospace companies of the missile age.

Radar

In 1947, Hughes Aircraft entered the low bid and received an Army Air Force contract to produce the APG-33 radar for use in all-weather fighters. This was an improved light-weight version of the APG-3 that had been developed by General Electric late in the Second World War. Hughes was taking a big gamble, as the company had little know-how when it came to producing radar sets, but it served to beome established in the then infant field of radar and electronic fire control.

Shortly afterward, Hughes Aircraft received a contract from the newly-created U.S. Air Force to modify the Sperry A-1 computing gunsight for use with the APG-33. In the summer of 1948, when the Cold War threatened to heat up, the Air Force rushed this system, called the E-1, into production on the Lockheed F-94A.

The Lockheed F-94 was this nation's first operational all-weather jet interceptor. It was a two-seater derived from the Air Force's TF-80 trainer. Unfortunately the radar system was so quirky and unreliable, that the crew members could never be sure that if it was working at the beginning of a flight, or that it would still be functional at the end.

The Falcon (GAR-1)—the first air-to-air missile to enter operational service in any Air Force — was developed and produced by the Hughes Aircraft Company. It weighed 100 lb. and carried a 29-lb. warhead using a semi-active radar homing technique, in which the launching aircraft's radar transmitter tracked the target and the missile homed in on radar waves reflected back from the target. (USAF, courtesy Norman Polmar)

"I propose to take all of the funds, profits, from my enterprises and found a great laboratory and attract the most eminent scientists in the world and give them ideal facilities with which to work."

— *Howard Hughes to General Ira C. Eaker*

World's Largest Helicopter

Experimental Sky Crane

In January 1946, Army Air Forces Materiel Command requested qualified manufacturers to submit proposals for the development of a large experimental helicopter, intended for use in the transfer of ordnance, equipment, supplies, and personnel. The bidders submitted proposals for a two-phase program consisting of a design study, followed by the production of a flying test-rig. The Kellett Aircraft Corporation of Upper Darby, Pennsylvania, won the design phase and was awarded a contract to build the test-rig for the XR-17 helicopter after the design was approved by the Air Force.

Hughes Buys the Kellett XR-17

While the XR-17 ground test-rig was under construction, Kellett ran into financial difficulties and in 1948 sold the rights for the partially completed rig — which was by then designated the XH-17 — to Hughes Aircraft for $250,000. To save costs on the program, Hughes incorporated several components into the XH-17 test-rig from other aircraft. These included the cockpit from a Waco CG-15, the landing gear from a North American B-25 and a Douglas C-54, and the fuel cell from the bomb bay of a Boeing B-29.

In October 1949 Hughes Aircraft was awarded a follow-on contract to modify the ground rig into a flying test-stand, and the XH-17 made its first flight on 23 October 1952. It was cut short after the huge helicopter had been airborne for barely a minute after Gale Moore, on the test flight, experienced excessive directional control forces acting on the craft. Also on board was Chal Bowen, who had been Hughes's flight engineer on the historic flight of the HK-1 Hercules. Both airmen had been paid $15,000 each to make the tests. No American insurance company would insure them, and the two pilots eventually obtained such protection from London. There was apprehension about the propulsion and control systems but these defects were quickly corrected. Other problems with the design were uncovered in subsequent trials but these could not be solved before the rotor blades reached the end of their design life, thus ending the program in December 1955.

Howard Did Not Fly

This aircraft would never have earned prizes for elegance. It could be described as a giant contraption, and it was the only Hughes airplane that Howard never flew. The U.S. Army funded its development and perhaps did not wish to risk the life of such a famous, and very rich man. In any case, Howard was not a helicopter pilot. Chal Bowen remembers the test flights that he made were hazardous but not excessively so. He felt that he more than earned the additional danger-money that was paid to him.

Top Right: This picture gives some idea of the size of the XR-17. (Chal Bowen)

Bottom Right: Howard (with Lucky Hat) is seen here, with a group of his staff and an Air Force representative, and the intrepid XR-17 crew. Chalmer Bowen is second from the right. (Chal Bowen)

Below: The XR-17 in flight. (Chal Bowen)

Hughes XH-17

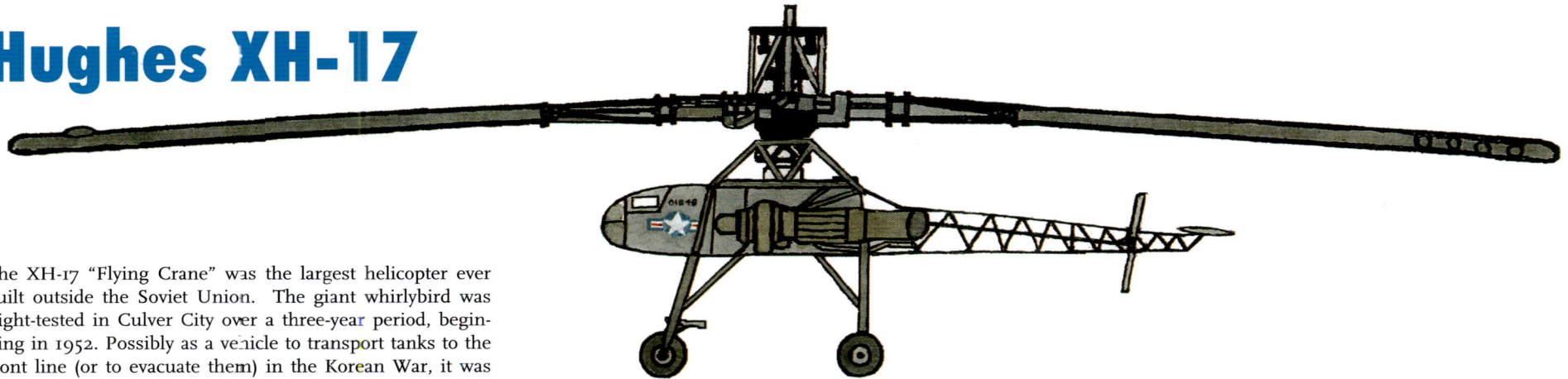

The XH-17 "Flying Crane" was the largest helicopter ever built outside the Soviet Union. The giant whirlybird was flight-tested in Culver City over a three-year period, beginning in 1952. Possibly as a vehicle to transport tanks to the front line (or to evacuate them) in the Korean War, it was designed to lift cargo weighing up to 24,700 lb. — more than ten tons and — almost half its total weight. To do so, it depended on a radically new form of lift power — two fuselage-mounted turbojets that provided enormous amounts of compressed air to pressure jets located on the blade-tips.

Piloting the Giant Helicopter

Pilot Gale Moore was an experienced helicopter pilot, having flown for Los Angeles Airways, a scheduled helicopter airline. Chalmer Bowen was the unofficial co-pilot, and wrote the instruction manual for this most unorthodox aircraft. At first, after firing up the engines, they would hold down the pitch to avoid hovering; then later, after much testing, they took off, demonstrating the XH-17 to the press and to the military. On one occasion, they "made a square" and even flew backwards.

As shown in the photograph, it was big enough to carry cars or trucks, and even a small tank. These would be driven on to a platform, secured on all four sides on the legs of the landing gear.

After the Korean War ended, there was no need for such an airlift. The project was scrapped and the engines were donated to the Northrop Training School.

End of Project

Although successful in its load-carrying ability, the extremely high fuel consumption of the two turbojets limited the aircraft's flight range to just 40 miles — far too little for the craft to be of much practical use. It could also be heard several miles away, and was thus severely handicapped for operations anywhere near the front line of battle.

Length	53 ft
Rotor Diameter	130 ft
Engines	General Electric J35 (5,600 lb. thrust) x 2
Number of Seats	2
Cruising Speed	60 mph
MGTOW	52,000 lb.
Max. Range	40 miles

Size comparison with Constellation (p.55)

The two cars and the man underneath the XH-17 give perspective to the ungainly-looking helicopter. Demonstrations were made, with cars driven up a ramp on to a platform supported by the four landing gear legs. (Chal Bowen collection)

The Supreme Piston-Engined Airliner

A Final Challenge

In 1952 T.W.A. began to operate an improved version of the Constellation, powered by four 2,700 hp Wright R-3350 engines. These Super Constellations (Lockheed Model 1049) had non-stop transcontinental range and were built to match the competition from Douglas DC-6Bs, giving T.W.A. a decided advantage in the domestic market. To counter the threat from the Super Constellation, American Airlines asked Douglas — which at the time was Lockheed's chief competitor in the U.S. and overseas markets for commercial transports — to develop an alternative to the 1049. The result was the DC-7, which first entered service in November 1953.

Before the Jets

When Hughes learned that Pan American Airways, T.W.A.'s chief rival on the Atlantic route, had requested Douglas to design a variant of the DC-7 that would be capable of regular non-stop Atlantic service (the 1049 had to stop for fuel when the winds were unfavorable) he turned to Lockheed once again, seeking to procure an airliner that would compete with the new Douglas DC-7C "Seven Seas." Lockheed responded by mating the Super Constellation's fuselage and tail surfaces with an entirely new wing, resulting in a major redesign. The outcome, the Model 1649A Starliner, entered service on 1 June 1957. Its Atlantic leadership was short-lived, however, because it was overtaken six months later, on 19 December 1957, by the faster, turbo-propeller-powered (prop-jet) Bristol Britannia 300, and by the jet-powered de Havilland Comet 4 and Boeing 707s in October 1958.

Lockheed Model 1649A Starliner

Lockheed had first responded to Hughes's request for a longer-range version of the Constellation with the 1449 design that was based around four PT2F-1 turboprop engines that Pratt & Whitney was developing. When it became apparent that the new engine would take too long to develop, Lockheed scrapped the turboprops in favor of conventional piston engines. Work on the new design, designated as the 1649 (later becoming the 1649A) began in May 1954.

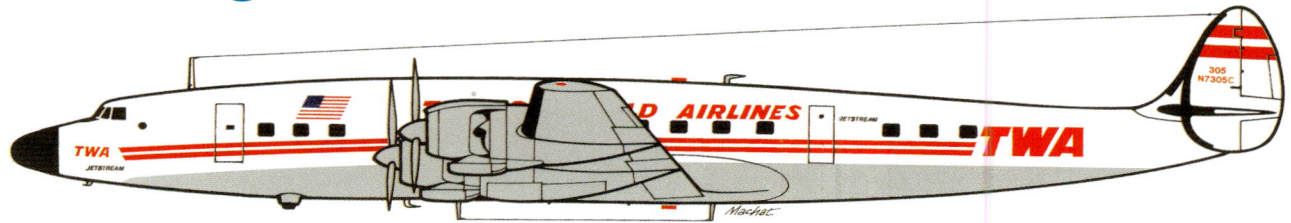

This fine long range piston-engined airliner was the ultimate development of the original Constellation, developed with Howard Hughes's personal contribution. (see pages 52–55)

Length	116 ft
Wing Span	150 ft
Engine	Wright R-3350-998TC (3,400 hp) x 4
Top Speed	376 mph
Cruising Speed	342 mph
MGTOW	156,000 lb.
Max. Range	4,000 miles

Size comparison with Constellation (p.55)

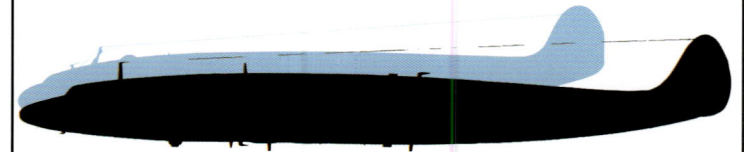

At first, it was called the Super Star Constellation, but the name was changed to the shorter, better sounding Starliner. The longer wing, which had almost twice the fuel capacity of the first Connie, gave the Starliner a range of more than 5,000 miles — nearly double that of the standard Connie. With its extended range, the Starliner could reach any western European capital non-stop from any U.S. city east of the Mississippi.

THE LOCKHEED CONSTELLATIONS COMPARED

	Length	Wing Span	Cruise Speed	MGTOW	Passengers (max.)	Normal Range (Full Payload)
049 Constellation	95 ft	123 ft	311 mph	86,250 lb.	51	2,500
649 Constellation	95 ft	123 ft	327 mph	94,000 lb	64	2,500
749 Constellation	95 ft	123 ft	300 mph	107,000 lb	64	3,000
1049A Super Constellation	114 ft	123 ft	301 mph	120,000 lb	64	3,500
1049G Super Constellation	114 ft	123 ft	355 mph	137,000 lb	92	3,500
1649A Starliner	116 ft	150 ft	342 mph	156,000 lb	88	4,000

Howard Hughes sponsored the ultimate development of the famous Lockheed Constellation series, the 1649A Starliner. It was almost twice the all-up weight and had almost twice the range of the original Model 49 (C-69) that he delivered to the government in 1944. (see page 52)

Avro Canada C102

The Avro Canada C-102 Jetliner

Ever alert to aeronautical progress during the early 1950s, and especially to any developments that might affect the fortunes of his airline, T.W.A., Howard Hughes kept a watchful eye on what was going on, not only in the States but elsewhere in the world. As well as being involved in building the giant XH-17 helicopter, described in previous pages, he was acutely conscious of the dawn of the Jet Age in commercial air transport.

As early as 10 August 1949, only two weeks after the de Havilland Comet made its historic maiden flight, Jimmy Orrell took off in the **Avro Canada C102** Jetliner at Toronto's Malton Airport. Designed by Jim Floyd and Guest Hake, it was for some time perceived as a rival to the Comet. As test flying continued, including some impressive test flights in January 1951 to Chicago, New York, Winnipeg, Tampa, and Miami, it attracted Howard's interest, even though T.C.A. (Trans-Canada Air Lines, later Air Canada) felt that it did not meet its requirements.

On 7/8 April 1952, Howard flew the C-102 to Culver City, where he flew it himself during most of the 13-1/2 hours of test flying for Hughes Aircraft. He returned the Jetliner to Malton on 30 September, and it made its last flight on 23 November 1956.

The Vickers Viscount

A year after the Comet made its debut with B.O.A.C., and before the metal fatigue-related disasters of early 1934, the world's first turboprop airliner, the **Vickers Viscount**, entered service with British European Airways on 16 April 1953. In September 1955, Howard sent a four-man team over to England to monitor the construction of one of these aircraft for his own use. The team stayed there for almost three years, but the aircraft was never delivered to Hughes, and was sold to South America. When the team came home, he turned his attention again to Canada, where T.C.A. had become the first airline in all the Americas to introduce a turbine-powered airliner. Whether or not Howard piloted the Viscount is not known for certain, but his flying time in Canada is another story, narrated on the next page.

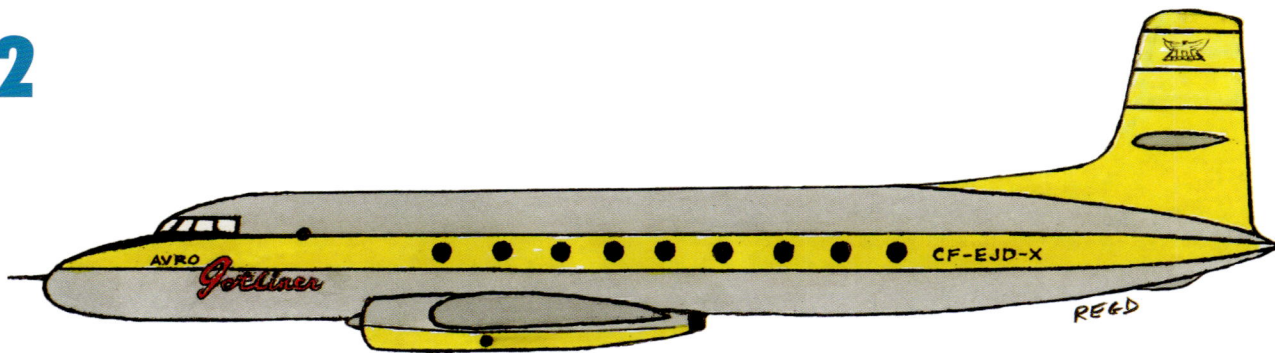

The Avro Canada C102 Jetliner came very close to making the first flight of any commercial jet airliner. Its first flight 10 August 1949 was only two weeks after the de Havilland Comet's dramatic debut on 27 July.

Length	81 ft
Wing Span	98 ft
Engine	Rolls-Royce Derwent (3,600 lb thrust) x 4
Seating	36
Cruising Speed	430 mph
MGTOW	65,000 lb.
Max. Range	1,800 miles

Size comparison with Constellation (p.55)

During a visit to Canada in the late 1950s, Howard may have had a chance to fly one of the Trans-Canada Air Lines Vickers Viscounts.

From April until September 1952, Howard Hughes borrowed the C102 Jetliner for his personal test-flying at Culver City.

This is the Britannia company demonstrator, G-ANBJ, flown to the United States in 1956 and demonstrated to Howard Hughes in Montreal.

The One that Got Away

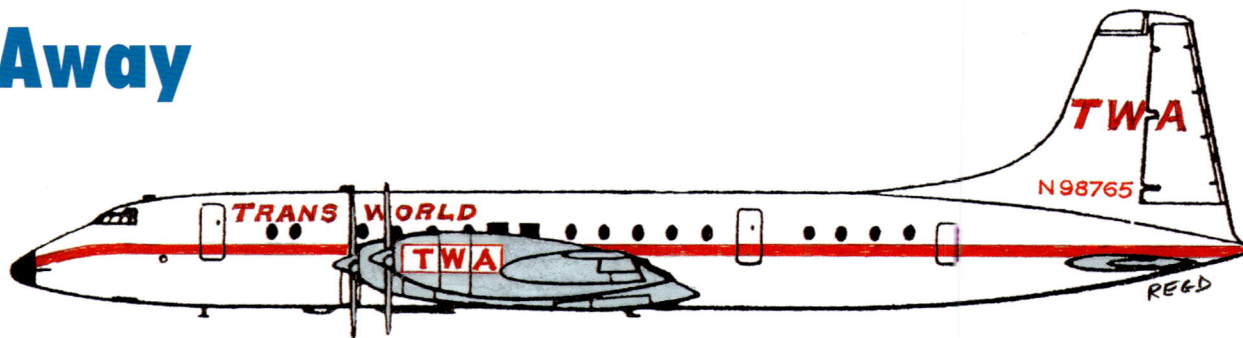

This drawing is the artist's impression of what the Bristol Britannia would have looked like in T.W.A. colors.

T.W.A. Crisis

Late in June 1957, Howard appropriated a brand new Model 1649 — the second off the production line — and flew it to Montreal with an entourage of his staff. The trip was ostensibly made to test-fly two British turboprop airliners: the short-range Vickers Viscount and the longer range Bristol Britannia. But Howard had just fired Noah Dietrick, his business aid, and faced tremendous financial hurtles as he tried to raise the $400 million needed to pay for the new jets, which T.W.A.'s competitive airlines had already ordered.

Rendezvous in Montreal

Arriving in Montreal, Howard got in touch with **Peter Masefield**, Managing Director of the Bristol Airplane Company, which had brought the Britannia with a Bristol air crew to help the sales effort. During long telephone conversations, Howard stated that he was interested in the airplane and wanted to take a look at it. "When can we expect you?" Masefield asked, not knowing that Hughes was in Montreal. "I'll knock on your door in five minutes," Hughes replied. He was one floor above Masefield, in the same hotel.

Still the Pilot

After looking at the brochures that Masefield had brought with him, Howard said that he would "like to look at the airplane and then tomorrow I'd like to take it up." So in the evening Howard was given a set of operating manuals so that he could become better acquainted with the airplane. He went into the Britannia's flight deck, and must have been up most of the night, because the cockpit light remained on long after everyone else had gone to bed.

At breakfast the next morning, dressed as usual in casual attire and sneakers, he reiterated the he wanted to fly the airplane. As he entered the cockpit, Bristol's chief pilot gestured Howard to the right hand seat inviting him to take the seat as co-pilot.

"No," exclaimed Howard, "I said I want to take it up and I'll be in the left-hand seat."

"With all due respect sir, this is a turboprop airplane with which you may not be as familiar as with piston engined airplanes; the reactions to the controls are sometimes very different and you might care to take the right hand seat first."

Length	124 ft
Wing Span	142 ft
Engine	Proteus 765 (4,450 hp) x 4
Top Speed	420 mph
Cruising Speed	385 mph
MGTOW	185,000 lb.
Max. Range	3,750 miles

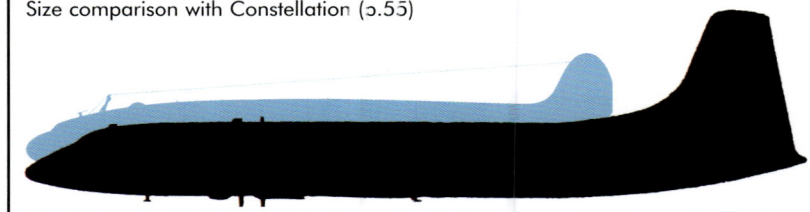

Size comparison with Constellation (0.55)

Hughes was adamant, "No I'll take it." He proceeded to fly the Britannia, making a series of take-offs and landings as if he had been flying the airplane for years.

When the Bristol team arrived back in Bristol everybody wanted to know what it was like to meet Howard Hughes, thinking that they would say "Oh, he's just a playboy, an eccentric, and you can't deal with him." Instead, the crew reported that although he was a man who was used to being completely in charge, he was also friendly, and was completely competent. They were absolutely in awe of Howard Hughes. They had seen him in action and realized that here was a man who was not only wished to sink many millions of dollars into his airplanes, he owned the airline that was going to buy it, and he could actually fly the airplane as well.

After the flight Hughes decided to buy a dozen of the turboprops, provided that Bristol could deliver the airplanes by April of the following year. But British airliner production standards were far removed from the disciplined assembly lines in America. In spite of manipulating the delivery positions of other airlines, they could not, and that was the end of the deal. Even so, Howard's financial resources were not what they were, and Bristol could have been gambling on the prestige benefits in selling to a U.S. airline.

Designed to a 1947 specification, and as a sequel to the recommendations of the wartime Brabazon Committee, the Bristol Britannia was a medium-range airliner. The prototype made its first flight on 16 August 1952. A long-range version, the Series 300, was developed for trans-Atlantic service. Entered service with B.O.A.C. on the London-New York route on 19 December 1957. El Al's neat slogan "No Goose, No Gander" (referring to the hitherto essential airfield staging and refuelling points in Labrador and Newfoundland), supported the Britannia claimed to be the first trans-Atlantic airliner that could fly non-stop in both directions with full payload in all seasons. This photograph, of G-ANBJ, was taken during a demonstration tour of North America and was the aircraft in which Howard Hughes made his practice runs.

Airline Swan Song

T.W.A. in Distress

In 1945, Howard Hughes had been obliged to borrow $30 million from the **Equitable Life Insurance** giant to keep T.W.A. afloat. In 1956, **Ralph Damon**, his experienced and reliable president died, and subsequently the airline was almost like a ship without a sail. Desperately needing jet equipment to meet the transcontinental and trans-Atlantic competition, by 1958, T.W.A. could not meet its payroll. Even the hitherto source of capital, the Hughes Tool Company did not have the resources, and a deal was made with Equitable, which had underwritten a $300 million jet procurement plan. But there were strings attached. In 1960, Hughes signed a $319 million financing plan, but only on condition that his stock was placed in a voting trust. A long-drawn out battle for control ensued, culminating with Howard's capitulation in 1966. He sold his 77% T.W.A. stock, at $86 per share, for $566 million, in about 20 minutes

Still the Airline Man

For a while, Howard Hughes went metaphorically into hibernation. Many airline and industry observers could not believe that he could stay away from aviation for very long — and they were right. Howard did not reveal his intentions after being ejected from the airline that he felt that he had nurtured for almost 30 years. It was a bitter blow. He must have taken the disappointment to heart, and made plans to re-enter the airline scene.

Air West

Knowing that the door was closed to regain control of, or even an interest in, T.W.A., he looked elsewhere. In 1968 he began to negotiate secretly with Nick Bez, chairman and C.E.O. of Air West, who, it was revealed during the later period of negotiations, was acting on behalf of Hughes the whole time. **Air West** was a newly-formed airline that had started operations under that name on 1 July 1968, when it was formed by the merger of three local service airlines: **Bonanza Air Lines** in Phoenix, **Pacific Air Lines** in San Francisco, and Bez's own **West Coast Airlines** in Seattle. On paper, the merger created an impressive regional air carrier, but it was under-capitalized.

Early in August, Howard formulated a master plan to acquire the airline, not, as Bez advised, by purchasing its stock, but rather through the purchase of its assets — a complicated move dictated by Hughes's special tax needs. The success of Howard's plan hinged on bad news for the airline. "The plan," as he explained Robert Maheu, "necessitates that we come along with a specific offer to pay the stockholders in liquidations a price substantially above the market. Any rise in the market before our offer will adversely affect the plan."

Hughes Negotiates

When the Air West board met in San Francisco in September 1968, Howard's offer was to acquire Air West's assets and assume all liabilities; in return the stockholders would receive cash payment of $22 per share, provided that the net worth of the airline had not decreased by 75 percent at the time of the sale. Howard's offer was approved by the board at the stockholders meeting on 27 December 1968. The next day the directors reversed themselves, when Northwest Airlines offered a better deal that did not involve purchase of the assets — just the stock. Howard fought back with a legal technique that his lawyers had used in the T.W.A. case. They filed a lawsuit in Delaware on behalf of the stockholders and asked the court — only permissible in Delaware — to seize the stock of the dissident directors until the case was resolved. Many of them had a large portion of their net worth tied up in Air West and the lawyers believed that the directors would swing over to Hughes once their assets were placed in jeopardy.

The negotiations with Northwest ended at the moment when the lawsuit was filed. The price of the airline's stock took a nose dive the next day. The directors, already jittery over the stockholders' suit, feared that the investors were panicking because Hughes's offer had not been accepted. It was later discovered that Hughes had been manipulating the stock, leading to a $33 million settlement later on.

Hughes Air West

On 31 December 1968, thirteen of the directors, who had previously voted against Howard's proposal, recanted and voted for it. Six months later, in July 1969, the Civil Aeronautics Board approved the acquisition of Air West

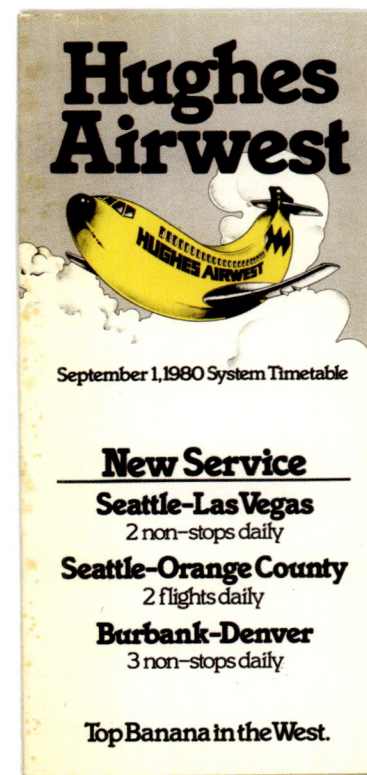

This was the last timetable issued by Hughes Airwest. It covered 33 cities west of the Rockies; 2 in Alberta, Canada; Denver, Milwaukee and Houston; and 3 resorts in Mexico.

by the Hughes Tool Company. On 31 March 1970, a new corporation, the Hughes Air Corporation, was formed, and in July of that year Air West was renamed Hughes Airwest. As before, Howard injected fresh capital into the new airline through the Hughes Air Corporation, 78 percent of which was owned by the Hughes Tool Company and 22 percent by Howard Hughes himself. By the time the Hughes name appeared on the side of an airliner, he was 70 years old, far from his former self, was terminally ill and did no flying. He may have had the ambition to expand Hughes Airwest to national airline status, but this will never be known. By the 1970s, the airline was being run by his Summa Corporation's staff, with Howard only an absentee figurehead.

The Hughes Legacy

Aviation Hall of Fame

Howard Hughes is remembered as a millionaire, epic movie-producer, Hollywood play-boy, eccentric loner, and the man who made the "Spruce Goose." First and foremost, however, he was one of America's great aviators. He once held every speed record of consequence and was hailed as the world's greatest flyer, "a second Lindbergh." At various points in his life he owned an international airline, two regional airlines, and an aircraft company. He could also fly, as a pilot, any of their airplanes. Despite the lack of formal training, he was also a superb, instinctive aeronautical engineer, who contributed significantly to the design of many airplanes. Howard's many accomplishments and contributions to U.S. aviation were formally recognized by his induction into the National Aviation Hall of Fame on 14 December 1973.

Aviation Awards Bestowed upon Howard Hughes
The Collier Trophy
The Chanute Award
The Congressional Medal
Two International Harmon Trophies

"Howard Hughes was a modest, retiring, lonely genius often misunderstood, sometimes misrepresented and libeled by malicious associates and greedy little men. But, his personal contributions to U.S. aviation, as test pilot, aeronautical engineer, airline executive, scientific laboratory founder, sponsor of aerospace education plus his philanthropic contributions and his patriotic dedication have earned him a place in this Great Aviation Hall of fame.

— General Ira C. Eaker, USAAF (ret.)

The H-1 Racer

Howard's cherished Racer was meticulously maintained and stored in a fenced-in area of a temperature-controlled hangar at Culver City for more than 30 years. It was fully refurbished in 1975 when it was donated to the National Air and Space Museum in Washington, D.C. where it remains today. It is fitting that the H-1 — an aircraft that had a major impact on the high-performance aircraft throughout the 1930s — is prominently displayed in the center of the Museum's exhibit on the Golden Age of Aviation. No other aircraft of that era exhibited the number or quality of outstanding design features that were incorporated into the H-1.

THE HK- 1 HERCULES

The Hughes-Kaiser HK-1, which is popularly known as the "Spruce Goose," — a name detested by Howard Hughes — remains the largest aircraft in terms of wingspan to have ever taken to the air. It is also the largest wooden airplane ever flown.

After its one-and-only flight on 1 November 1947, Hughes placed the Flying Boat in its custom-built hangar and ordered her to be maintained in flight-ready condition. She remained in "hibernation" for 33 years at a cost of approximately one million dollars per year. In 1976, after Hughes's death, his holding company — the Summa Corporation — donated the aircraft to the non-profit Aero Club of Southern California, which then leased it to the Wrather Corporation. Wrather moved the flying boat to a site on Long Beach Harbor where it was opened to the public in 1983. It remained there until 1993, when it was moved to the Evergreen International Aviation Museum in McMinnville, Oregon, where it now serves as the centerpiece of their aircraft collection.

The Howard Hughes Medical Institute

The creation of the Medical Institute that bears his name stands as Hughes's most enduring accomplishment. It is the second largest philanthropic organization in the United States — only the Gates Foundation is larger.

Hughes created the Institute in the last hours of 1953 to solve a multitude of problems that he was then facing, including the ire of Secretary of the Air Force who was threatening to put the Tool Company's Aircraft Division out of business.

Dividing His Empire

On 17 December Hughes's attorneys set up two new corporations. One was the Hughes Aircraft Company, a separate company formed from the assets and liabilities of the Aircraft Division; the other was called the HHMI Corporation — a non-profit corporation set up with Hughes as its sole trustee. Its purpose, as stated in its incorporation papers, was "the promotion of human knowledge within the field of the basic sciences and its effective application for the benefit of mankind. The next day, the name was changed to the Howard Hughes Medical Institute.

This was a bold stroke of financial genius. By transferring all his stock of the Hughes Aircraft Company to the Institute, Hughes turned the large defense contractor into a tax exempt charity, preventing the loss of the company (Defense Department officials would think twice before canceling the contracts of a company owned by a company devoted to medical research "for the sake of mankind") and turning it into a tax heaven the would generate millions of dollars of revenue through payments from the Institute to the Hughes Tool Company. HHMI leased land and buildings from the Tool Company that would be used by Hughes Aircraft, which in turn would pay HHMI for the use of the property.

The Ultimate Charity

Without donating a single penny, Howard Hughes had created a public relations bonanza that was worth millions of dollars in income and tax deductions, for the Tool Company could deduct its lease payments to the medical institute on its federal income tax. Since the lease payments were part of Hughes Aircraft's cost of doing business, they in turn could be passed on to the United States government as part of the work it was doing on military contracts.

As Bartlett and Steel so aptly point out, Howard Hughes had created the ultimate charity: "the American taxpayer was to pick up the entire bill for the Howard Hughes Medical Institute, while Hughes basked in the warm glow of testimonials to his philanthropy and quietly collected money from his own charity."

Epilogue

When Howard Hughes died, he had founded three important aerospace corporations. These were:

Hughes Aircraft

Preeminent supplier of airborne radar, fire control,
and air-to-air missiles.

Hughes Helicopters

Major supplier of military helicopters.

Hughes Space and Communications Co.

One of the leading suppliers of space satellites
and communications systems.

He had still been flying airplanes until 1960, but thereafter he flew as a passenger until he briefly resumed flying himself in 1973. In 1972, Hughes sold the Hughes Tool Company and formed a holding company, named the **Summa Corporation**, to manage his remaining investments that included enormous real estate holdings, his electronics company, and Hughes Airwest — the regional airline that he acquired in 1970, as his last involvement in the airline business.

Increasingly reclusive, he visited the Bahamas and Mexico, accompanied by an entourage of Mormons who catered to his every wish. As was customary whenever Hughes traveled, his staff did not simply book a room; they booked a whole floor. He was also reported to have been involved in preliminary feasibility studies in Nicaragua, with the objective of surveying the route of a canal to rival that in Panama. As usual, he had rented the top floor of the leading hotel in Managua, but departed when a massive earthquake almost destroyed the city.

On 9 August 1973, while in London, ever avoiding the public and the press, he fell down the back stairs of the Inn on the Park hotel on Park Lane, and fractured his hip. Returning to the States, it is believed that he refused to have surgery, and his physical health, already declining and heavily dependent on drugs, began to deteriorate further.

By now a sad, sickened, shadow of the vigorous man that he once was, Hughes was by then utterly dependent on devoted help from a tolerant staff. In his declining years, he lent his name to the C.I.A., which built the *Glomar Explorer*, a specialized ship, packed with advanced technology, designed to recover a Soviet submarine that had sunk in the Pacific Ocean.

Right to the end, amid periods of illness, physical and mental, there were thus flashes of inspiration to reflect, albeit distantly, a creative mind. This period of his fading life ended after a flight to Acapulco in 1976. On 5 April of that year, in desperate need of medical attention, he died — appropriately as he would have wished — in an airplane, a private jet en route to Houston, where he was buried after a little-publicized funeral. He was 70 years old, and did not leave a will, which led to many complications for the administration of his estate, which comprised 26 operating companies in 16 different lines of business. Of these, Hughes Helicopters was sold to McDonnell Douglas for close to half a billion dollars — which helped to settle outstanding tax liabilities.

In 1994, the Summa Corporation was renamed **The Howard Hughes Corporation**, embodying the spirit of Hughes's vision and acumen in every aspect of its commercial, industrial, and residential developments. Early in 1995, the board of directors initiated a recapitalization process that culminated on 12 June 1996, in a merger with **The Rouse Company** of Columbia, Maryland, which was one of the largest publicly-held real estate development and management companies in the United States. Howard Hughes, The Aviator, was now only a distant memory.

Bibliography

Allen, Richard S. *The Northrop Story 1929-1939.* New York: Orion, 1990.

Baron, Charles. *Howard Hughes and His Flying Boat.* Fallbrook, Calif.: Aero Press, 1982.

Bartlett, Donald L. and James B. Steele. *Empire: The Life, Legend and Madness of Howard Hughes.* New York: Norton, 1979.

Brown, Harry P. and Pat H. Broeske. *Howard Hughes: The Untold Story.* New York: Dutton, 1996.

Cochran, Jacqueline and Maryann B. Brinley. *Jackie Cochran: An Autobiography.* New York: Bantam, 1987.

Corn, Joseph H. *The Winged Gospel: America's Romance with Aviation, 1900-1950.* New York: Oxford University Press, 1983.

Davies, R. E. G. "Howard Hughes," in *The Airline Industry* edited by William M. Leary. New York: Facts on File, 1992.

Davies, R. E. G. *Rebels and Reformers of the Airways.* Washington, D.C.: Smithsonian Institution Press, 1987.

Davies, R. E. G. *TWA: An Airline and Its Aircraft.* McLean, Va.: Paladwr Press, 2000.

Dietrich, Noah, & Bob Thomas. *Howard: The Amazing Mr. Hughes.* Greenwich, Ct.: Fawcett, 1972.

Dwiggins, Don. *Hollywood Pilot: The Biography of Paul Mantz.* New York: Doubleday, 1967.

Hack, Richard. *Hughes: The Private Diaries, Memos and Letters, The Definitive Biography of the First American Billionaire.* Beverly Hills, Calif.: New Millennium Press, 2001.

Frazer, Chelsa C. *Famous American Flyers.* New York: Thomas Y. Crowell Company, 1941.

Glines, Carroll V. *Roscoe Turner: Aviation's Master Showman.* Washington, D.C.: Smithsonian Institution Press, 1995.

Johnson, Clarence L "Kelly" with Maggie Smith. *Kelly: More Than My Share Of It All.* Washington, D.C.: Smithsonian Institution Press, 1985.

Keats, John. *Howard Hughes.* NY: Random House, 1966.

Matt, Paul. "Howard Hughes and the Hughes Racer," *The Historical Aviation Album.* Temple City, California: 1980.

McDonald, John J. *Howard Hughes and His Hercules.* Shrewsbury, UK: Airlife Publishing Ltd., 1983.

Miller, Ronald and David Sawyers. *The Technical Development of Modern Aviation.* London: Routledge and Kegan Paul, 1968.

Pisano, Dominick. *The Airplane in American Culture.* Ann Arbor, Michigan: University of Michigan Press, 2003.

Rummel, Robert W. *Howard Hughes and TWA.* Washington: Smithsonian Institution Press, 1991.

Scatzberg, Eric. *Wings of Wood, Wings of Metal: Culture and Technical Choice in American Airplane Materials, 1914-1945.* Princeton, NJ: Princeton University Press, 1998.

Serling, Robert. *Howard Hughes' Airline: An Informal History of TWA.* New York: St Martin's, 1983.

Smith, Henry L. *Airways: The History of Commercial Aviation in the United States.* Washington, D.C.: Smithsonian Institution Press, 1991 [Reprint].

Stringfellow, Curtis K. and Peter M. Bowers. *Lockheed Constellation: Design, Development, and Service History of all Civil and Military Constellations, Super Constellations, and Starliners.* Oscelola, Wisconsin: Motorbooks, 1992.

Special Collections

Howard R. Hughes Collection, Florida Air Museum, Lakeland, Fl.

Albert I. Lodwick Papers, Lakeland Library, Lakeland, Fl.

Sherman Fairchild Papers, Library of Congress, Washington, D.C.

Sara Clark Collection (U.S. Army Air Forces Research and Development Files), National Archives, College Park, Md.

Delmar F. Fahrney Collection (History of Guided Missiles), National Archives, College Park, Md.

Aircraft Files, National Air and Space Museum Archives, Washington, D.C.

American Institute of Aeronautics and Astronautics Archives, Library of Congress, Washington, D.C.

Engineering and Scientific Awards, Endowments, and Institutions named in memory of Howard Hughes that honor his pioneering accomplishments in aviation:

Howard Hughes College of Engineering (UNLV)

Howard Hughes Professor of Applied Physics and Material Science (Caltech)

Howard Hughes Award (Aero Club of Southern California)

Howard Hughes Award for Outstanding Improvement in Helicopter Technology (American Helicopter Society)

Howard Hughes Undergraduate Science Enrichment Program (UCSD)

Index

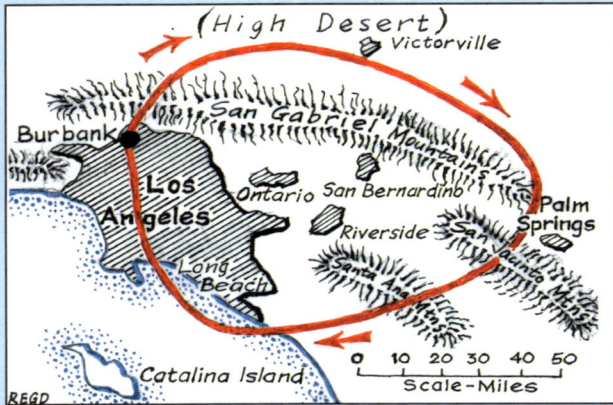
Page 22 (Practicing)

Page 30 (Testing)

Page 33 (Record Flight)

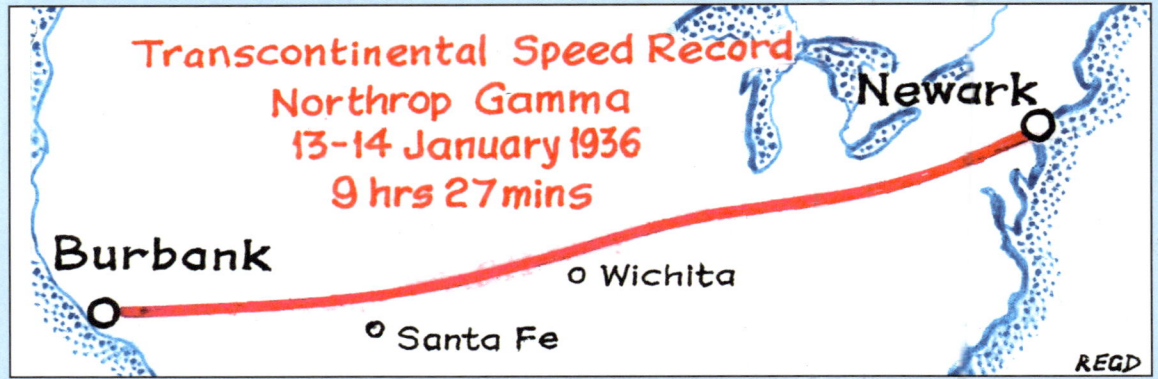

**Transcontinental Speed Record
Northrop Gamma
13-14 January 1936
9 hrs 27 mins**

Burbank — o Wichita — o Santa Fe — Newark

Page 30 (and 33) (Record Flight)

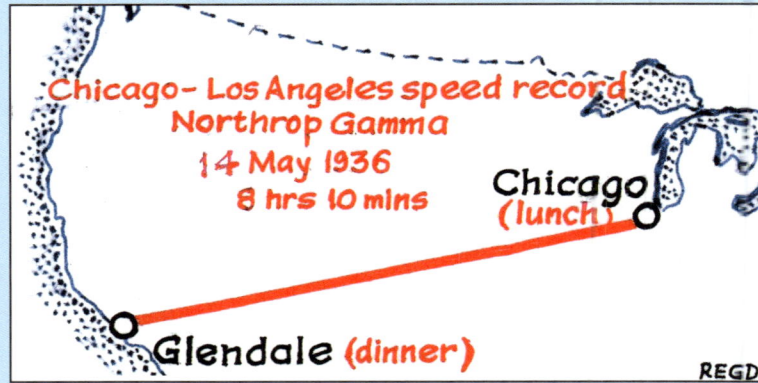

**Chicago- Los Angeles speed record
Northrop Gamma
14 May 1936
8 hrs 10 mins**

Chicago (lunch) — Glendale (dinner)

Page 33 (Record Flight)

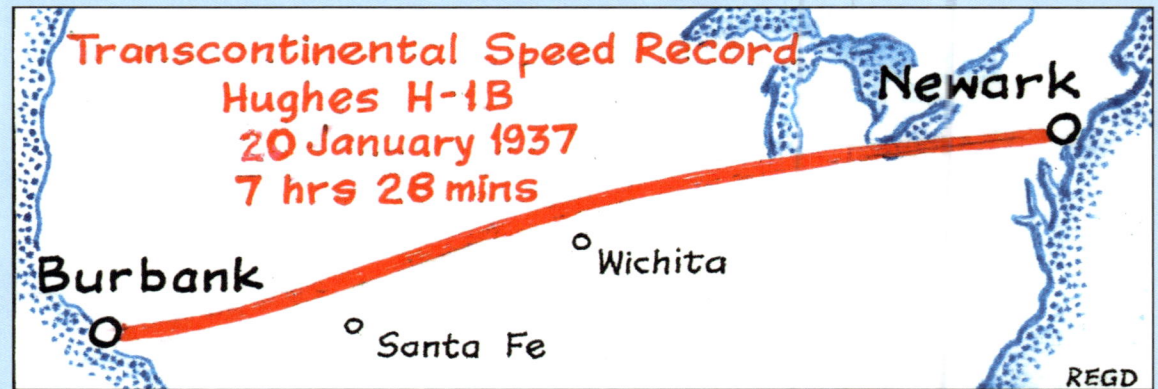

**Transcontinental Speed Record
Hughes H-1B
20 January 1937
7 hrs 28 mins**

Burbank — o Wichita — o Santa Fe — Newark

Page 33 (Record Flight)

A Phenomenal Flying Career, in Maps

During only eight years, Howard Hughes accomplished his ambition to be a great aviator, challenging Charles Lindbergh for this position in aviation history. In 1936 he set a new U.S. transcontinental speed record, and in 1937 beat his own record with his own Hughes Racer. In 1938 he beat Wiley Post's round-the-world record; he bought one of the world's great airlines in 1940; and in 1944 he delivered to the U.S. government one of the most famous airliners in airline history, one in which he had participated in its design and construction. On this last dramatic occasion, he had, uniquely, helped to design, owned, and flown the same aircraft.